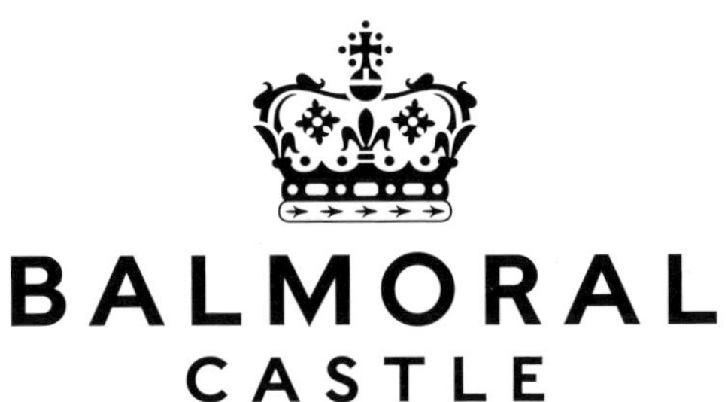

# BALMORAL
## CASTLE

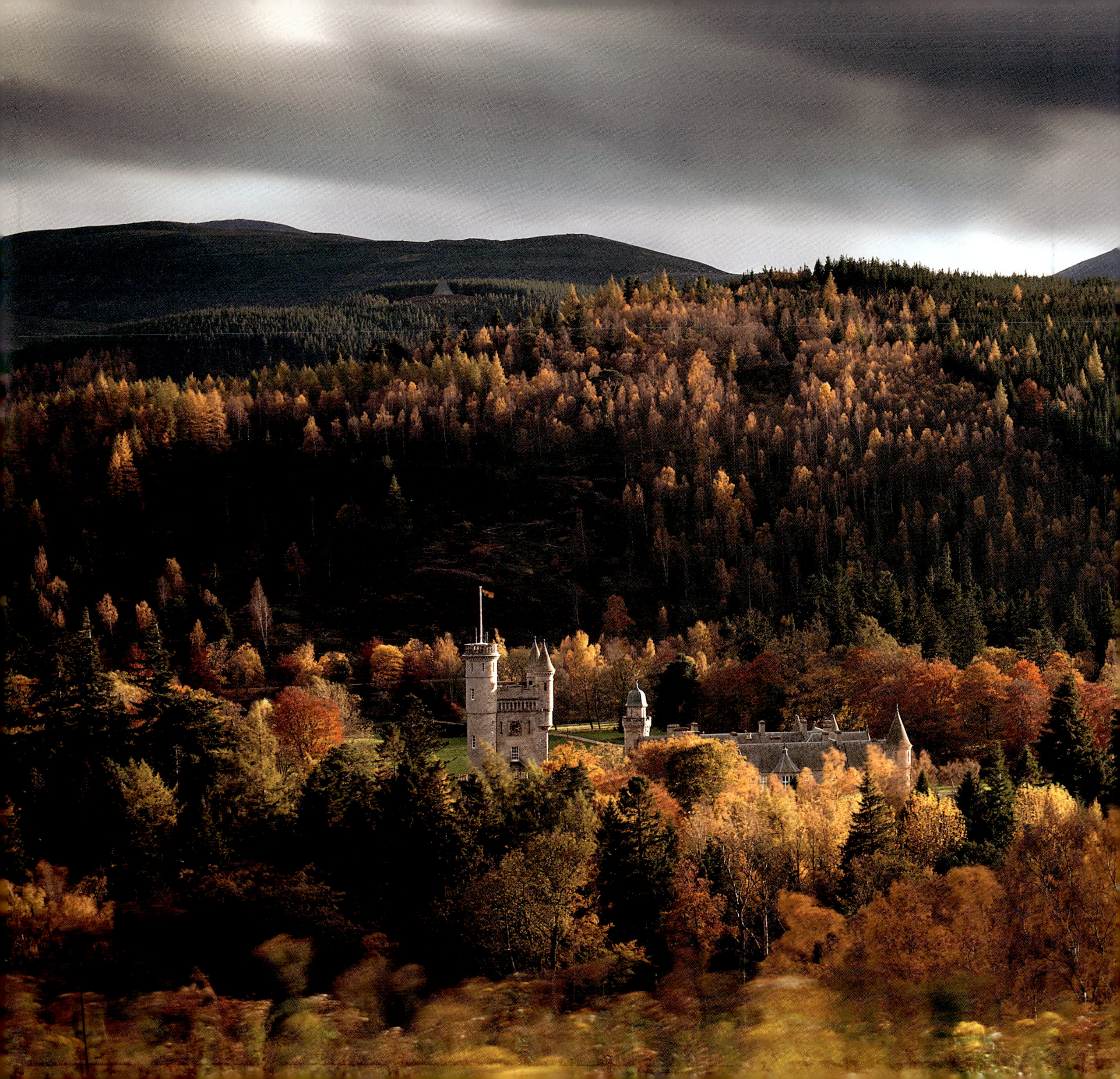

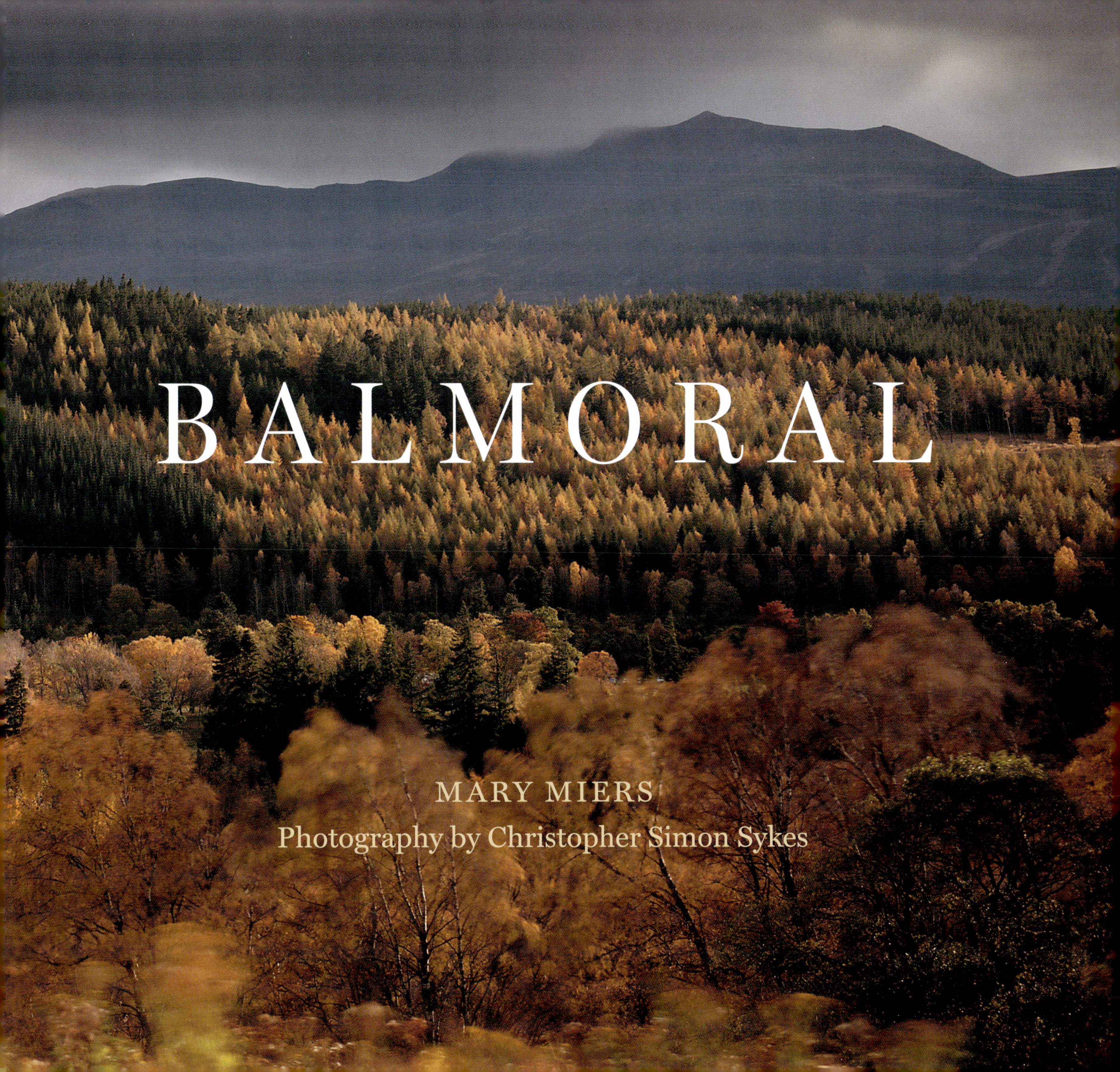

BALMORAL
MARY MIERS
Photography by Christopher Simon Sykes

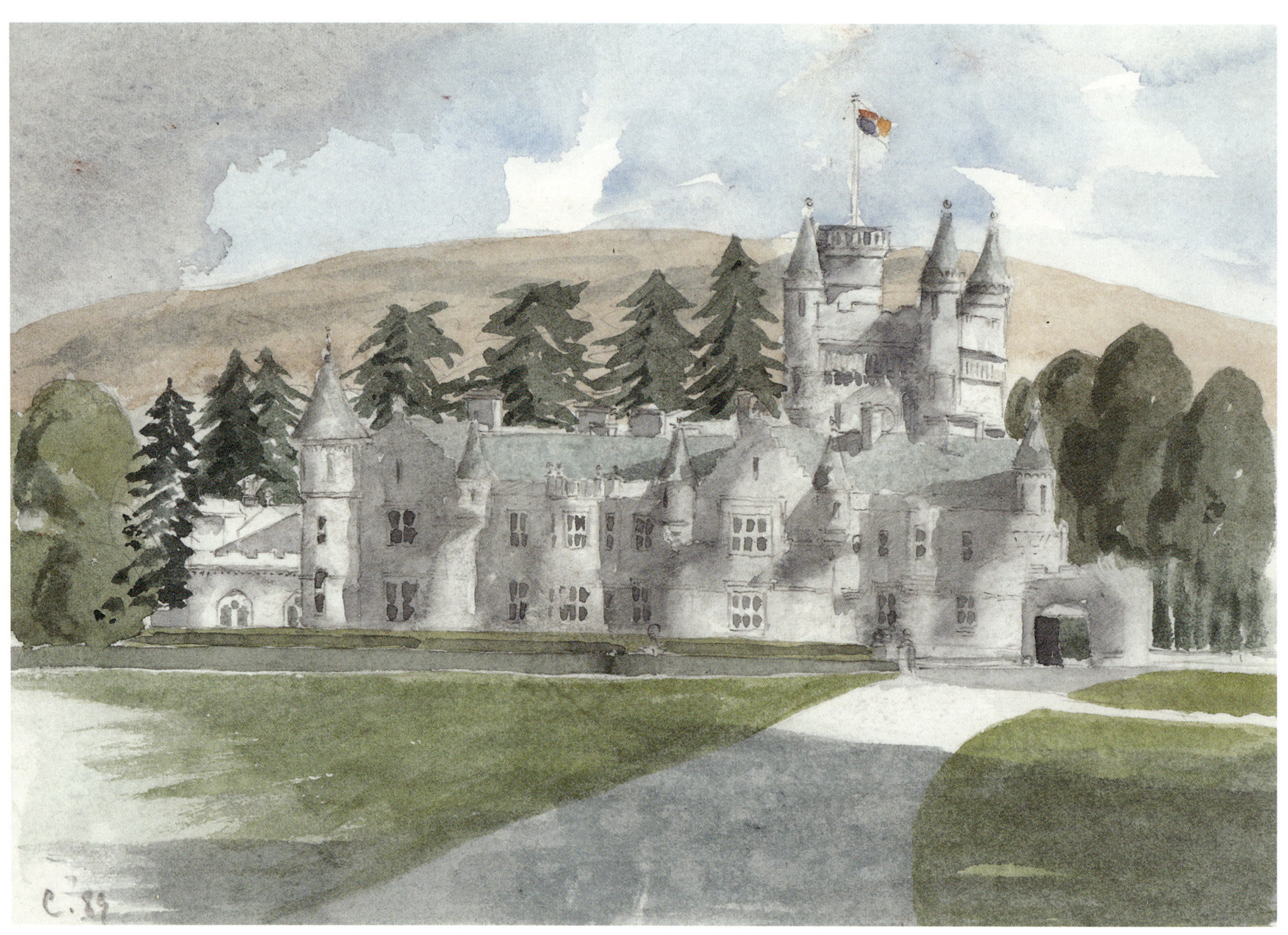

*Balmoral Castle, Aberdeenshire*, a watercolour by King Charles III,
painted in 1989 when Prince of Wales.

# Foreword

Balmoral has been the cherished Scottish home of my family since the estate was purchased by Prince Albert, my great, great, great grandfather, in 1852. With its buildings of startling individuality, which never fail to fascinate, and its precious, almost sacred, surrounding landscape, it is a place where there is constant change, yet everything remains unaltered, with a sense of timelessness which refreshes the soul.

Since my earliest childhood, it has held, and continues to hold, a uniquely special place in the hearts of my family and myself, and my late mother particularly treasured her time at Balmoral. It was here, in these most beloved of surroundings, that she chose to spend her final days.

Whatever the circumstances in which you are reading this book, I hope that you, too, will be inspired by the rich complexity of the architecture and share in the magic of the surrounding countryside, whose 'wild and majestic' landscape has been the source of inspiration and enjoyment for so many.

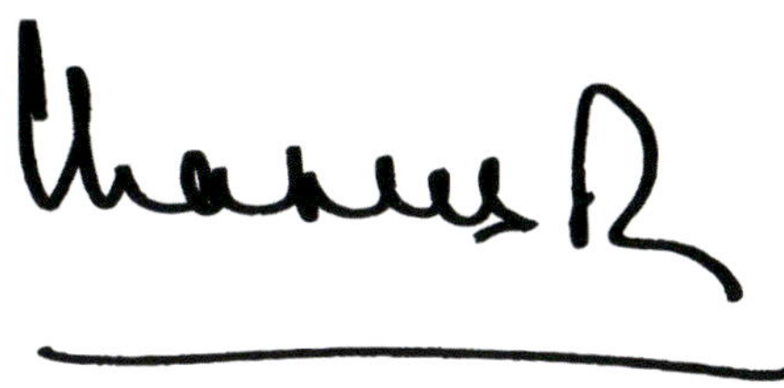

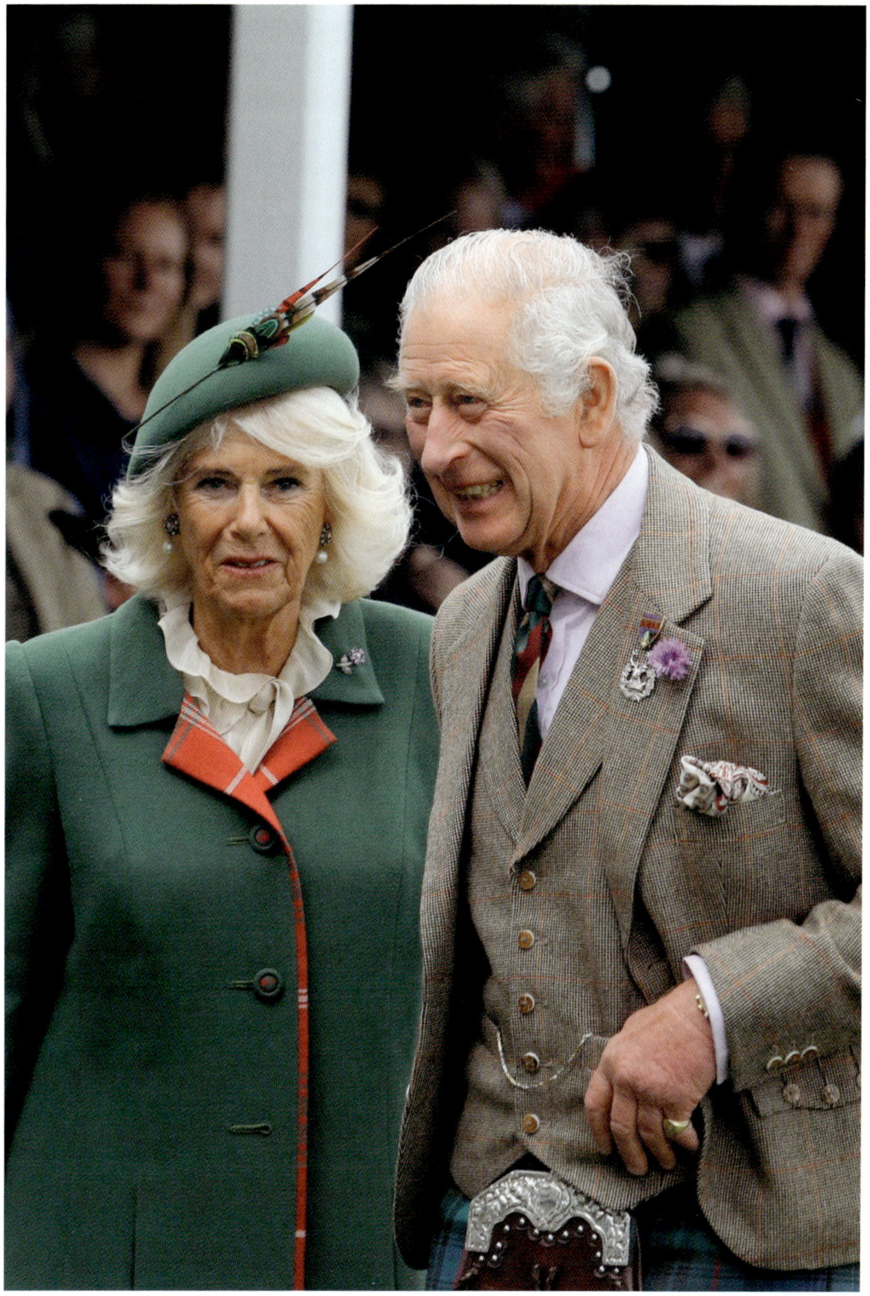

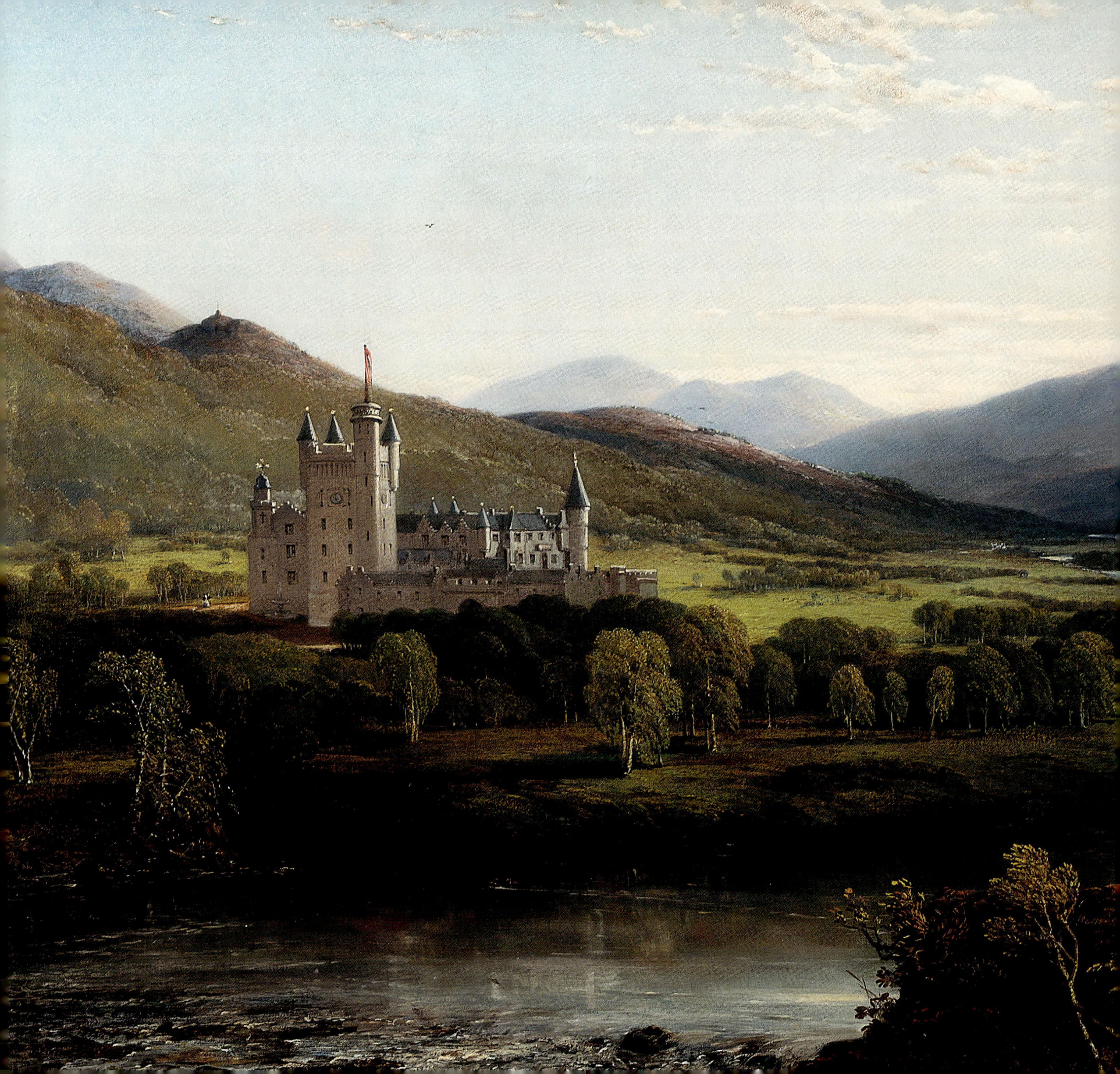

# Queen Victoria and Prince Albert: the Creation of Balmoral

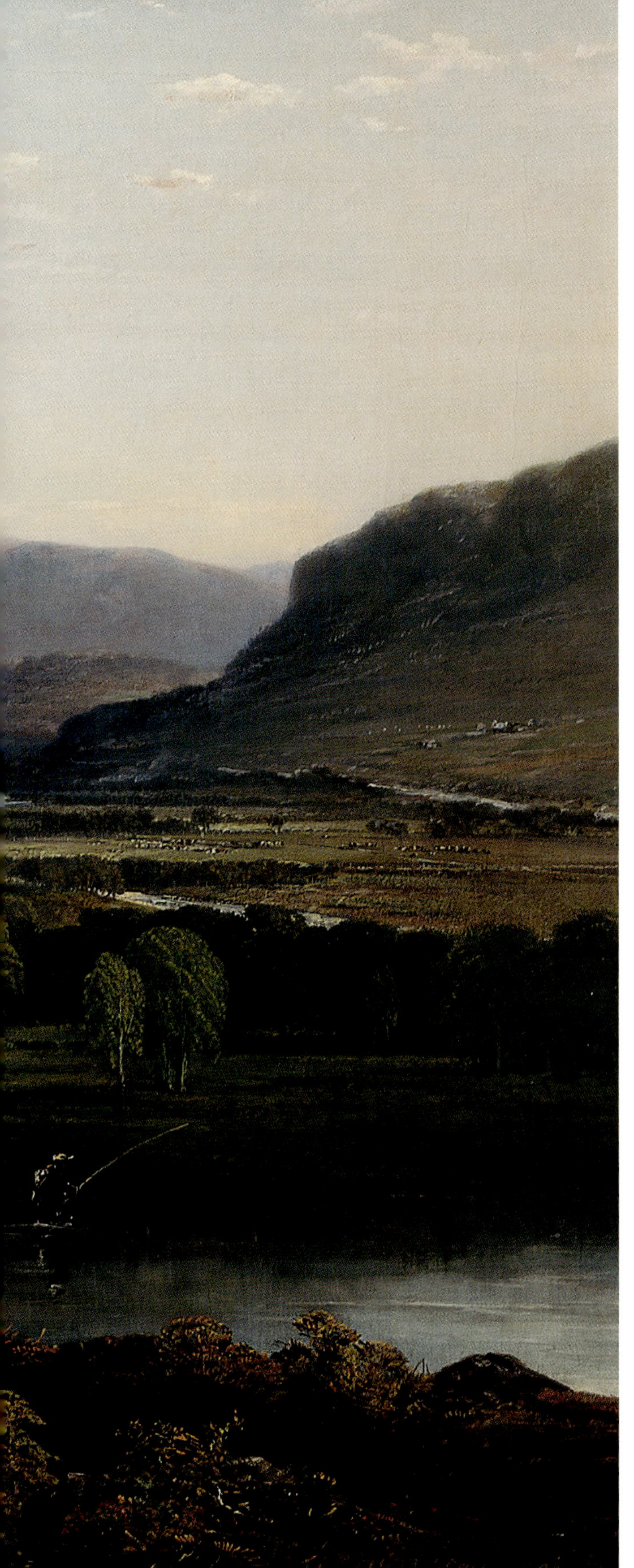

*left* Dating from between 1850 and 1874, this view by James Cassie RSA shows Balmoral Castle from the north east, looking across the Dee. The great, keep-like tower provides a stirring counterpoint to the principal rooms facing west up the Dee Valley and the lower service ranges to the fore.

When Queen Victoria and Prince Albert first came to Balmoral in September 1848, they were already captivated by the romanticised image of Scotland that had been popularised by their favourite author, Sir Walter Scott. The climax of their first northern tour, made in 1842 when they were both just 23, had been a three-day pageant of tartan-clad soldiers and pipers, fireworks, bonfires, Gaelic rowing songs, banquets and reels in the evocative setting of Taymouth Castle, which the Marquess of Breadalbane had remodelled for the occasion. 'It seemed as if a great chieftain in olden feudal times was receiving his sovereign,' the Queen enthused in her Journal; 'It was princely and romantic.' The Prince Consort, who had grown up at his father's Gothicised Rosenau Castle near Coburg, wrote that 'Scotland has made a highly favourable impression upon us both … Every spot is connected with some interesting historical fact, and with most of these Sir Walter Scott's accurate descriptions have made us familiar.'

Two subsequent visits, including a few weeks living 'a somewhat primitive, yet Romantic mountain life' at Blair Castle and a wet and midge-ridden month isolated in a shooting lodge on Loch Laggan, had strengthened the couple's resolve to find a Highland retreat of their own. The Royal physician, Sir James Clark, reported on Deeside's unusually dry and healthy climate and some watercolours were commissioned from James Giles to show enticing views of the scenery. They had already set their sights on the region when Sir Robert Gordon, who had leased

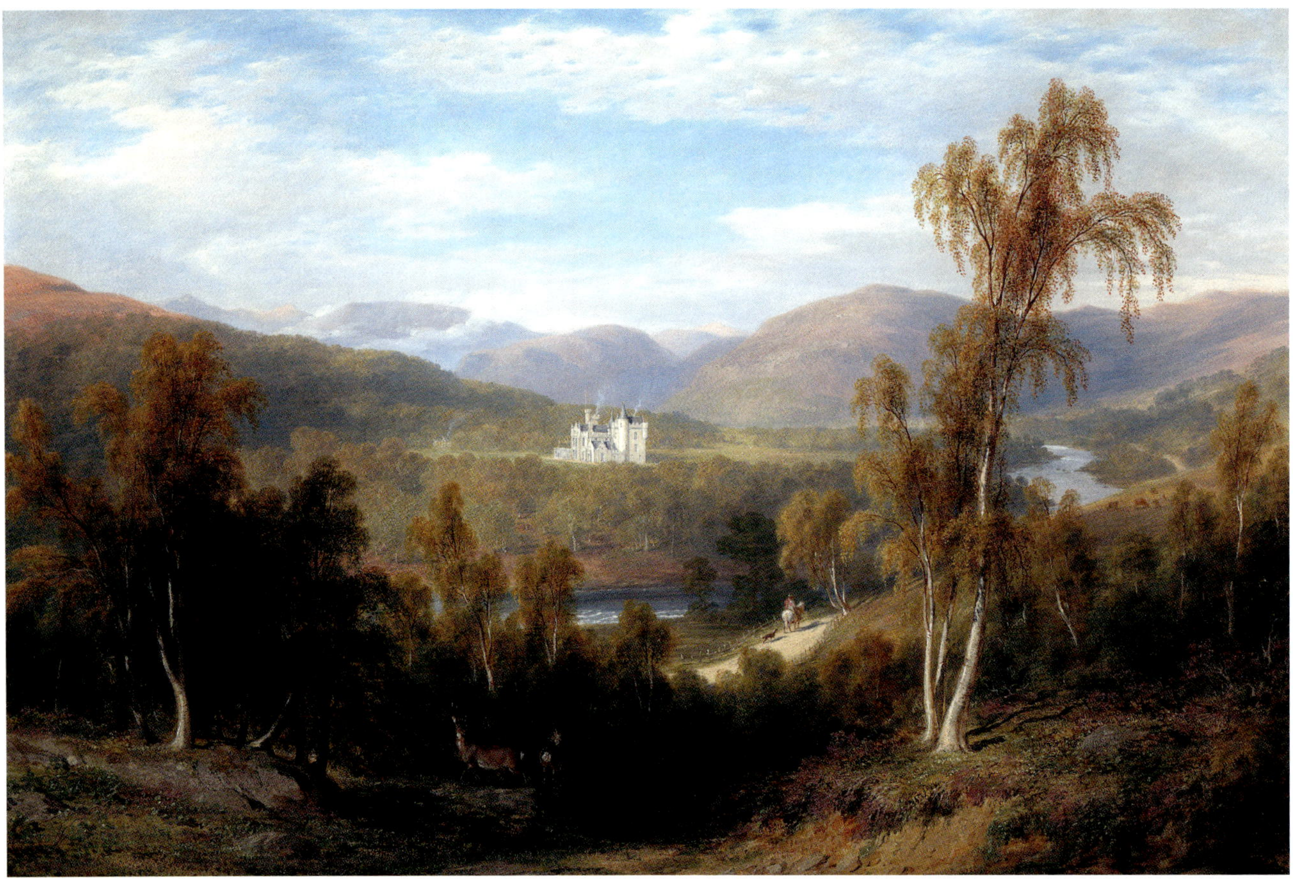



*left* *A View of Balmoral Castle* by James Giles, 1848, showing the old castle from the north east. Enlarged by John Smith of Aberdeen in 1834–39, the building was demolished in 1856, leaving just a stone marking the site of its front door, 100 yards south of the present castle.

Balmoral since 1830, choked on a fishbone and died. This misfortune left the estate in need of a new tenant and, in February 1848, Prince Albert agreed to take the lease, sight unseen.

Balmoral lies on the south side of the Dee, centred on a wooded strath within a curve of the river between Ballater and Braemar. Inaccessible to north and south except through the treacherous mountain passes of the Cairngorms, it was held by various Gordons until 1662, when it passed to a cadet branch of the Jacobite Farquharsons. In 1798, they sold Balmoral to the 2nd Earl of Fife, whose vast holdings included the neighbouring lands of Mar. Thereafter, it was let on sporting tenancies, the longest held by

Sir Robert Gordon, who, between 1834 and 1849, transformed the late-medieval tower into a rambling house designed by John Smith of Aberdeen.

It was there that the Royal Family stayed as tenants for four summers, having been treated to an ecstatic welcome by the Deeside Highlanders when they first came in September 1848. The Highland Season was already well established, with wealthy 'Sassenachs' making the annual migration to partake in all the activities that the Royal Family now embraced. On their first holiday, they made expeditions to Ballochbuie Forest and ascended Lochnagar on stony tracks, accompanied by the head keeper, gillies and grooms, the Queen on her pony 'well wrapped up in plaids'. Albert shot ptarmigan and his first Balmoral stag and they sketched and admired the Falls of Garbh Allt.

They were intoxicated by the wildness, the silence – 'excepting that of the wind or the call of the blackcock or grouse' – and the bracing air. Deeside, with its fast-flowing river and mountains fringed with pinewoods, reminded them of Albert's native Thuringia and offered a respite from the formality of Royal life and the political and social upheavals that were shaking Europe. While the Chartist Riots dominated news back home, in the far north and west, potato famine, disease and the Highland Clearances were decimating the glens and the Church was in the throes of a bitter disruption. Deeside was less drastically affected, but the Queen, who took an active interest in the tenantry and visited their dwellings, was not oblivious to the poverty. Nevertheless, Balmoral 'seemed to breathe freedom and peace, and make one forget the world and its sad turmoils'.

In June 1852, following protracted negotiations with the Fife trustees, the purchase of the estate was finally completed in Albert's name.

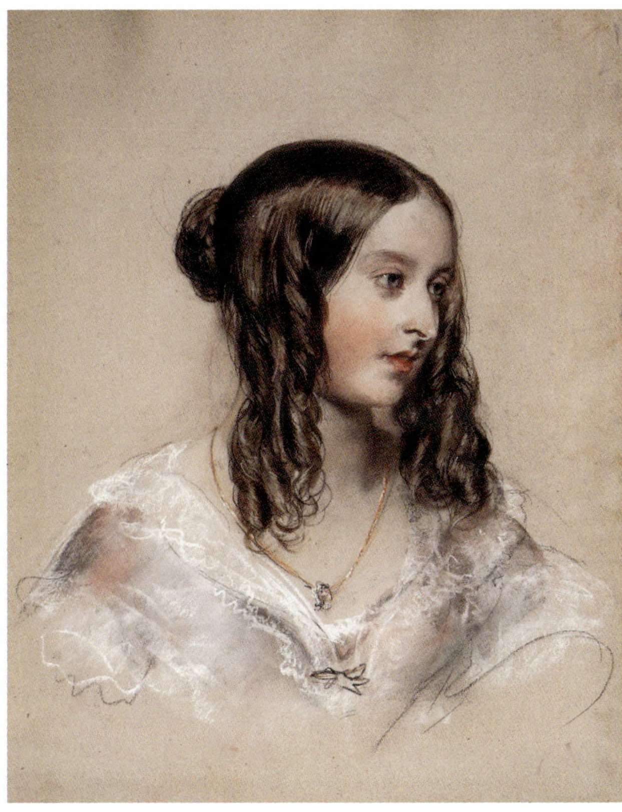

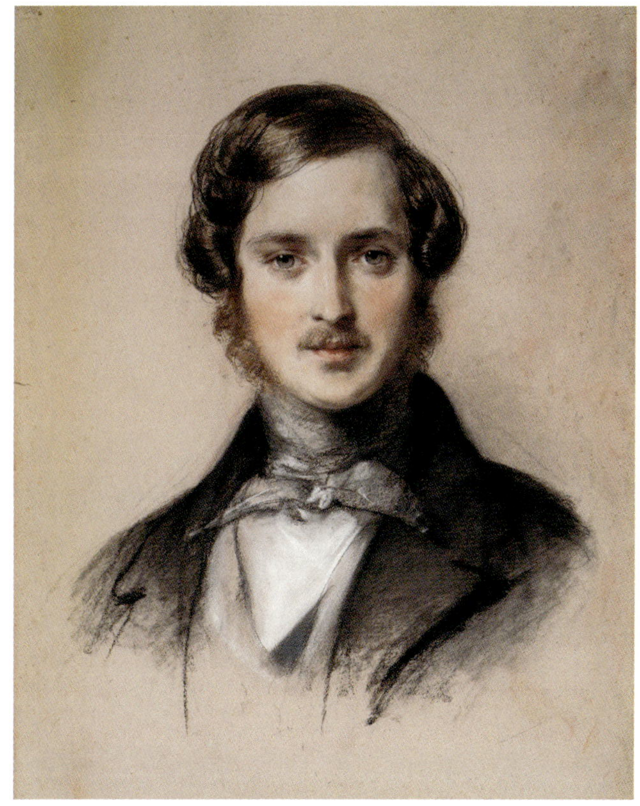

*right* Queen Victoria (1819–1901) and Prince Albert (1819–61) were newly married when the Hungarian artist Charles (Károly) Brocky made these beautiful chalk portraits, now in the Small Dining Room. Dating from 1841, they capture the youth and vitality of the couple shortly before they first came north and fell in love with Scotland.

Having decided against a scheme to extend the old house, he now approved drawings by William Smith (who had succeeded his father as Aberdeen City Architect) for a new building closer to the river. The Queen laid the foundation stone on 28 September 1853.

Albert's role in the creation of Balmoral was all-encompassing. Deeply interested in architecture, sciences and the arts, he collaborated on the design and supervised the detail with methodical precision. His Italianate taste had been given picturesque expression at the other holiday home he had recently built: Osborne in the Isle of Wight. For his next project, he was 'very much afraid of getting out of the rough character of a Highland residence'.

Architecturally and decoratively, the new castle borrowed elements from the old: the Scots-Tudor detail; the arrangement of the great square tower with circular stair turret in homage to the original keep; the picturesque massing when viewed from certain angles. With its towers and turrets, crowsteps, crenellations and corbelling, and the armorial carvings set into finely tooled granite, new Balmoral undoubtedly did much to popularise Scotland's revivalist national style. Yet,

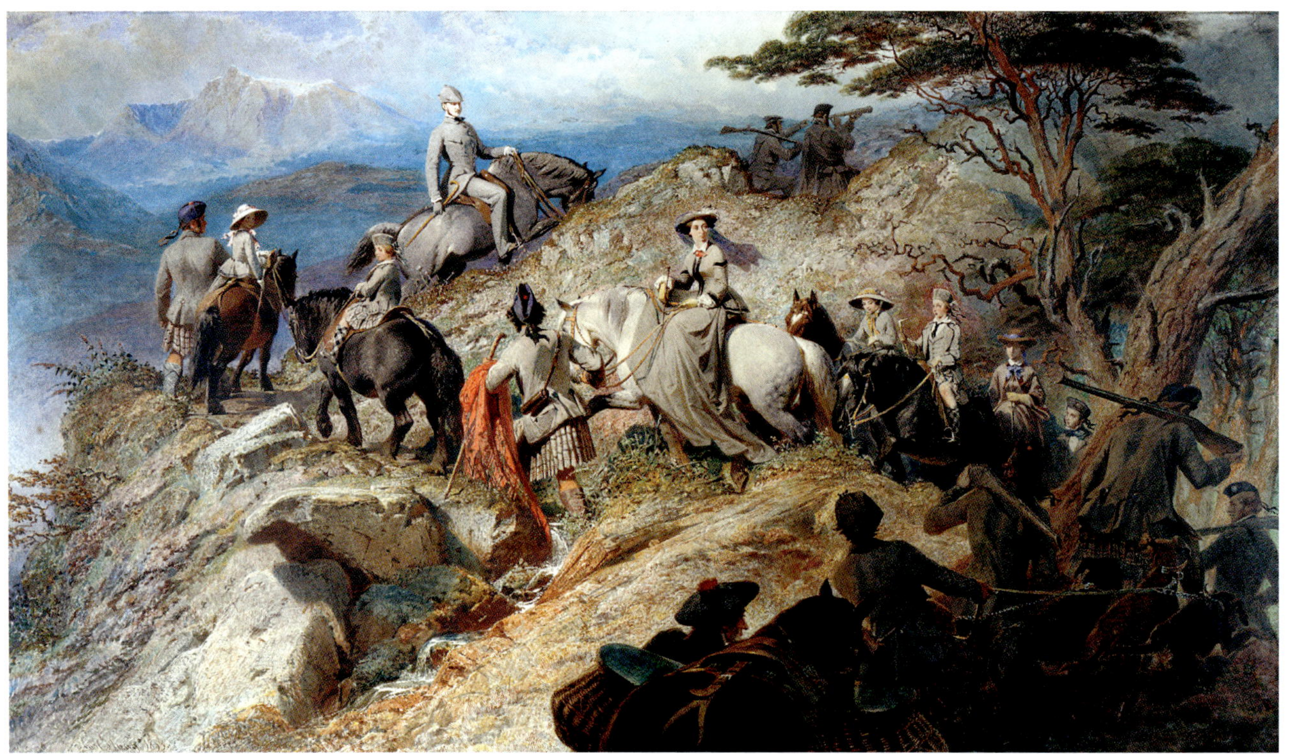



*left* Carl Haag's *Morning in the Highlands* sums up the love of the Cairngorms landscape and of being outdoors in the wilds. Painted with much input from Albert in 1853, and exhibited to acclaim at the Old Watercolour Society in 1854, it shows the Royal party setting out from Glenmuick to ascend Lochnagar, the mountain visible in the distance. It can be seen with its companion watercolour in the Small Dining Room.

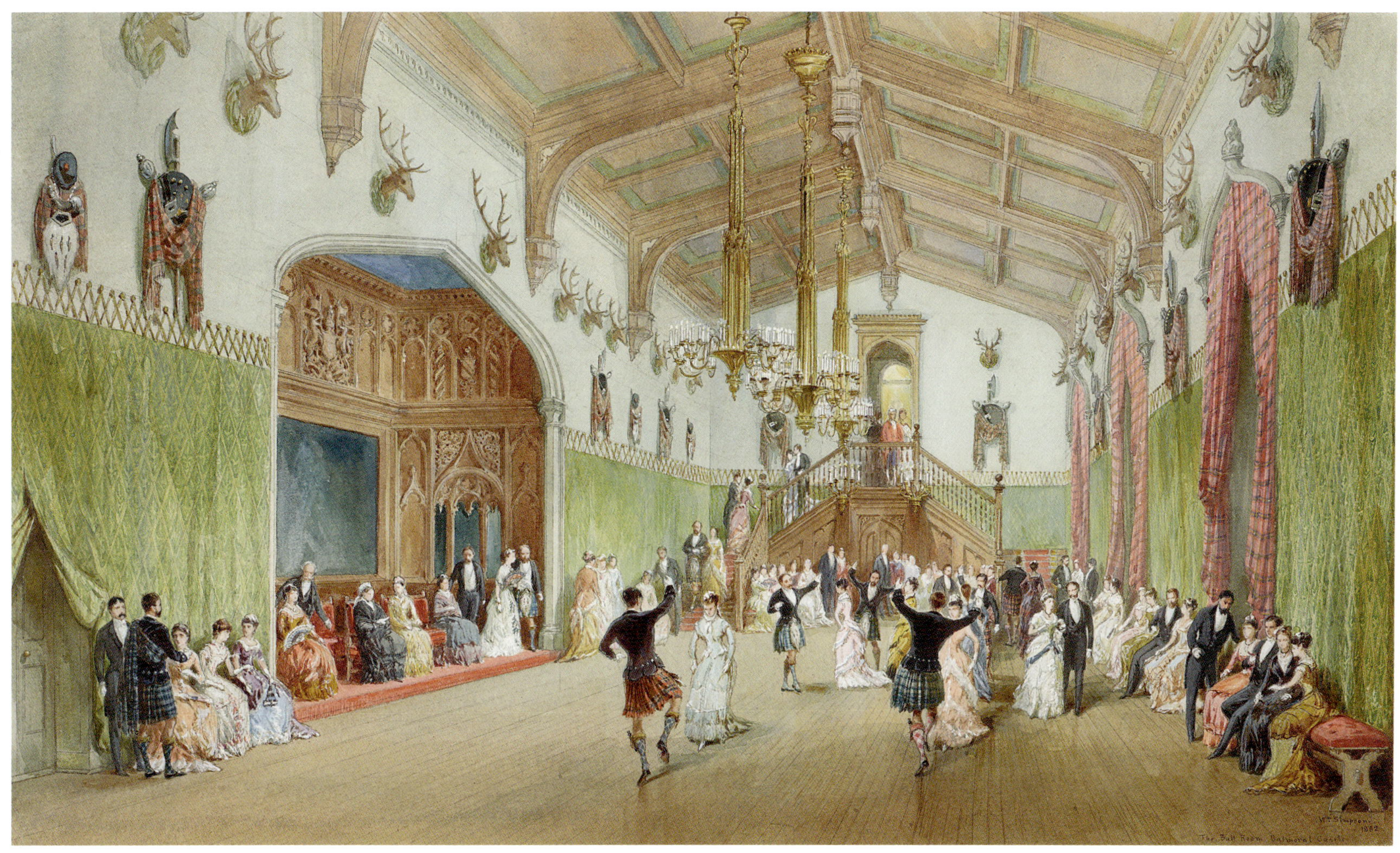



*above* The ballroom, seen here in William Simpson's watercolour of 1882, was decorated by the theatre designer Thomas Grieve as a fantasy Gothic hall. Royal Stewart tartan festoons the great windows and is draped over the sporrans, swords and targes displayed between stag-head trophies and silk hangings suspended from criss-cross cords.

architecturally, it was not so much full-blooded Scotch Baronial as an eclectic mix of Scots, English-Tudor and Germanic styles.

Balmoral's unprecedented scale and fine craftsmanship reflected the fact that this was the private Scottish home of the Sovereign as well as a Highland shooting lodge. The plan was logical and highly specialised, comprising two linked quadrangles – one containing the principal accommodation, the other the kitchen and domestic offices – set diagonally to each other to maximise views.

Almost everything inside was supplied by the leading London furnisher-decorators, Holland & Sons. They could work in any style, but here adopted a 'cosy, mid-century approach with a strong Scottish flavour' that belied Balmoral's status as a Royal residence. Tartan, combined with stencilled wallpapers and thistle-sprigged chintzes, created a cheerful sense of pattern and colour that was offset by pale woods and silvered metalwork. Some gently satirised the Scotch-themed decor, but the whole effect was a refreshing alternative to what would come

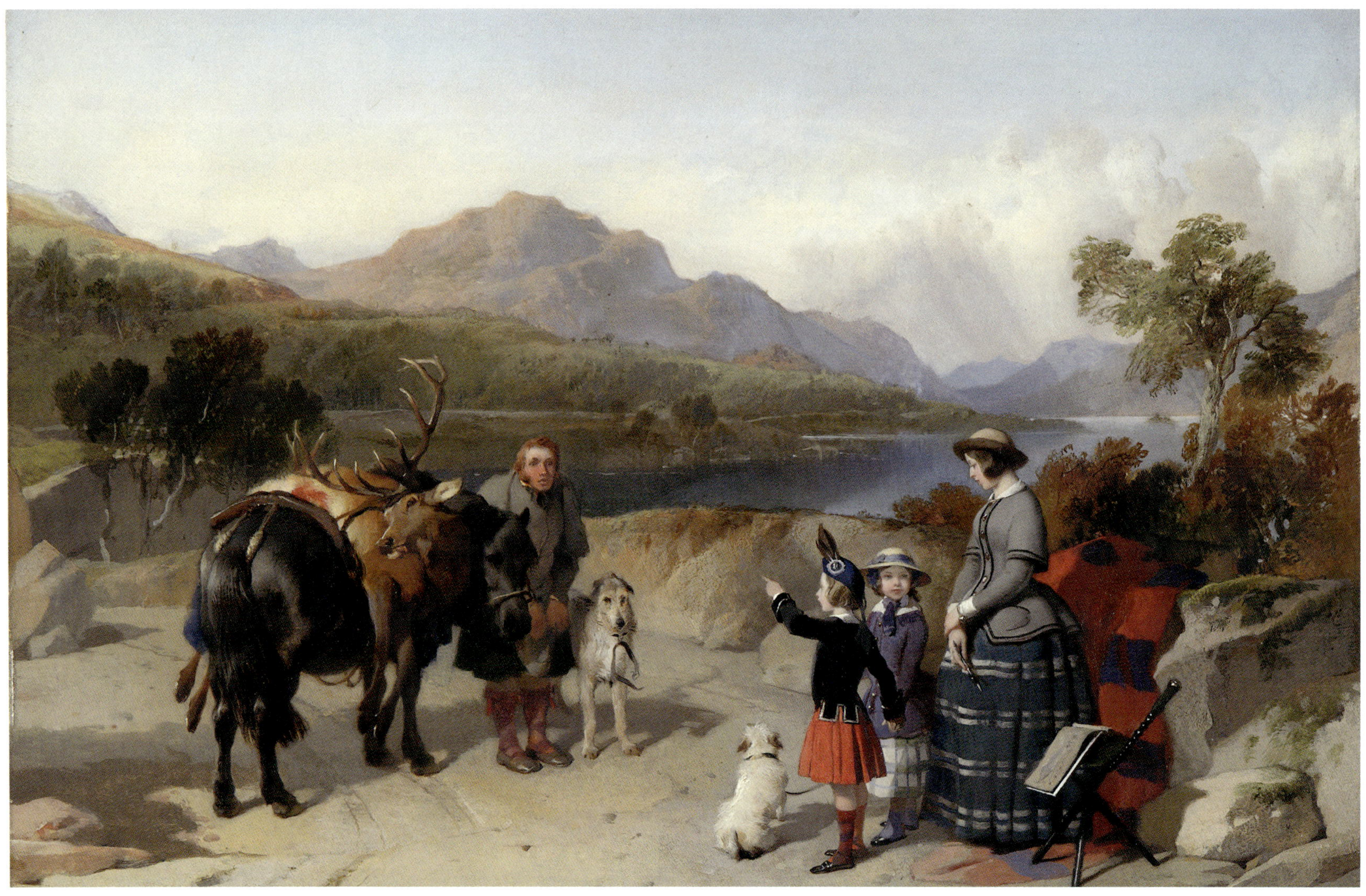

to be caricatured as the 'Bloodsports Baronial'. Taxidermy was confined to the entrance hall and corridors.

The family moved in on 7 September 1855, just hours after the decorators had finished fitting up the main rooms. For a while, the two buildings stood side by side, but the old castle was finally demolished in 1856.

Visitors commented on the lack of pomp and the relative informality of Royal holidays at Balmoral. Life revolved around picnics and boating, hill walks and sketching trips, shooting and fishing, gillies' balls and Highland games, as featured in the Queen's famous Souvenir Albums and other scrapbooks. Each year, a professional artist was invited north to record the views and activities and sometimes give lessons. The watercolourist William Leitch recalled 'the joyous bustle in the morning when the Prince went out; the highland ponies and

*above* Landseer's *Queen Victoria Sketching at Loch Laggan* was conceived when he visited her at Ardverikie in September 1847. Begun in November, it was painted in a hurry, with secret visits to Windsor to capture the likenesses, so that Victoria could give it to Albert for Christmas.

In 1857, the drawing master James Roberts made 12 watercolours of the new interiors, six of which survive in the Royal Collection. They provide the best record of the original decoration.

*above* Tartan and thistles are the keynotes of the Queen's bedroom, with its Brussels carpet in Hunting Stewart and a Balmoral tartan plaid on the table. Thistles sprig the 'Balmoral' chintz and form a running pattern along the canopy and the green wallpaper is stencilled with gold fleurs-de-lis. Holland & Sons supplied everything, including the bed and its hangings (costing £169 12s 11d) and the maplewood furniture.

*below* A Royal Stewart carpet, Dress Stewart curtains and upholstery, and blue wallpaper stencilled with gold and white thistles offset the drawing room's white marble chimneypiece, pale woodwork and mostly satinwood furniture. Thistles decorate the chair backs, door handles and fireplace tiles. Pictures, framed '*en-suite* with the furniture in pale wood', are limited to stalking and animal engravings after Landseer.

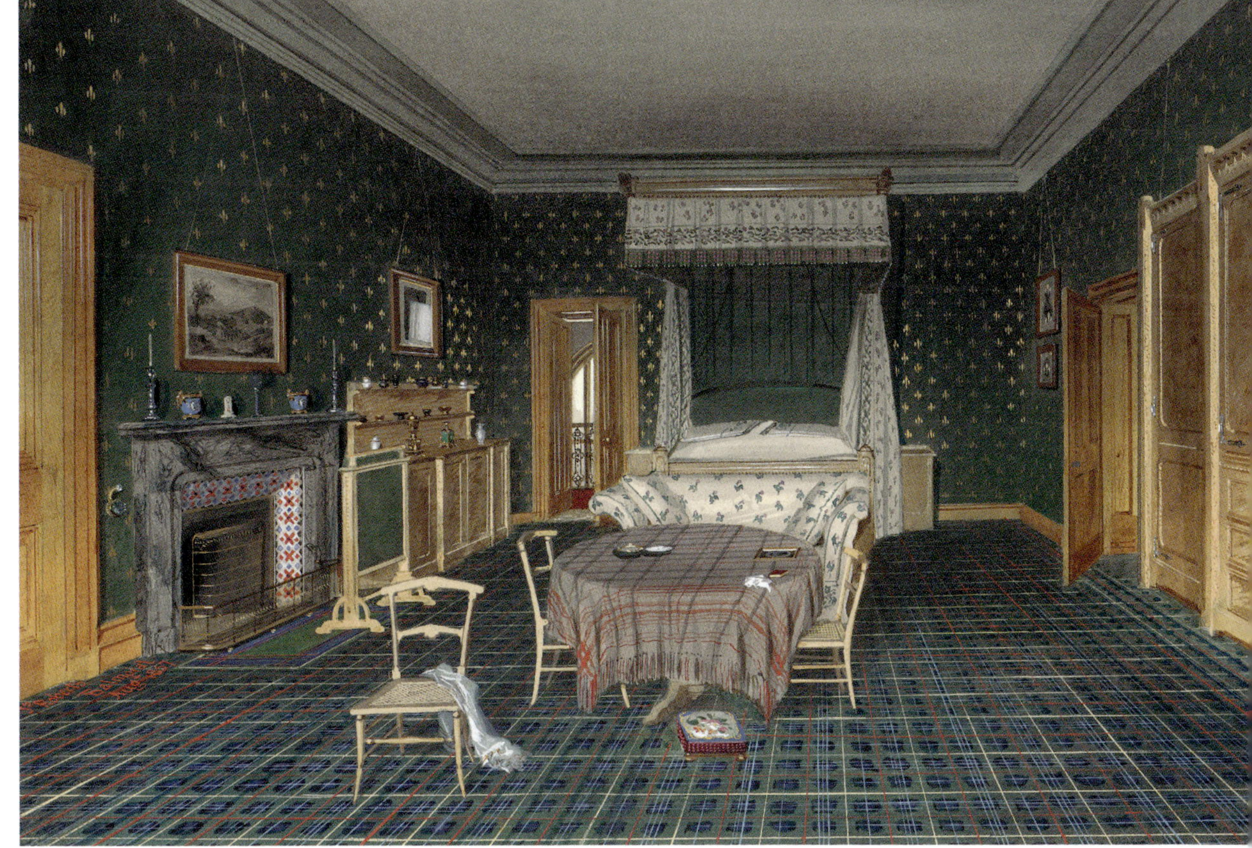

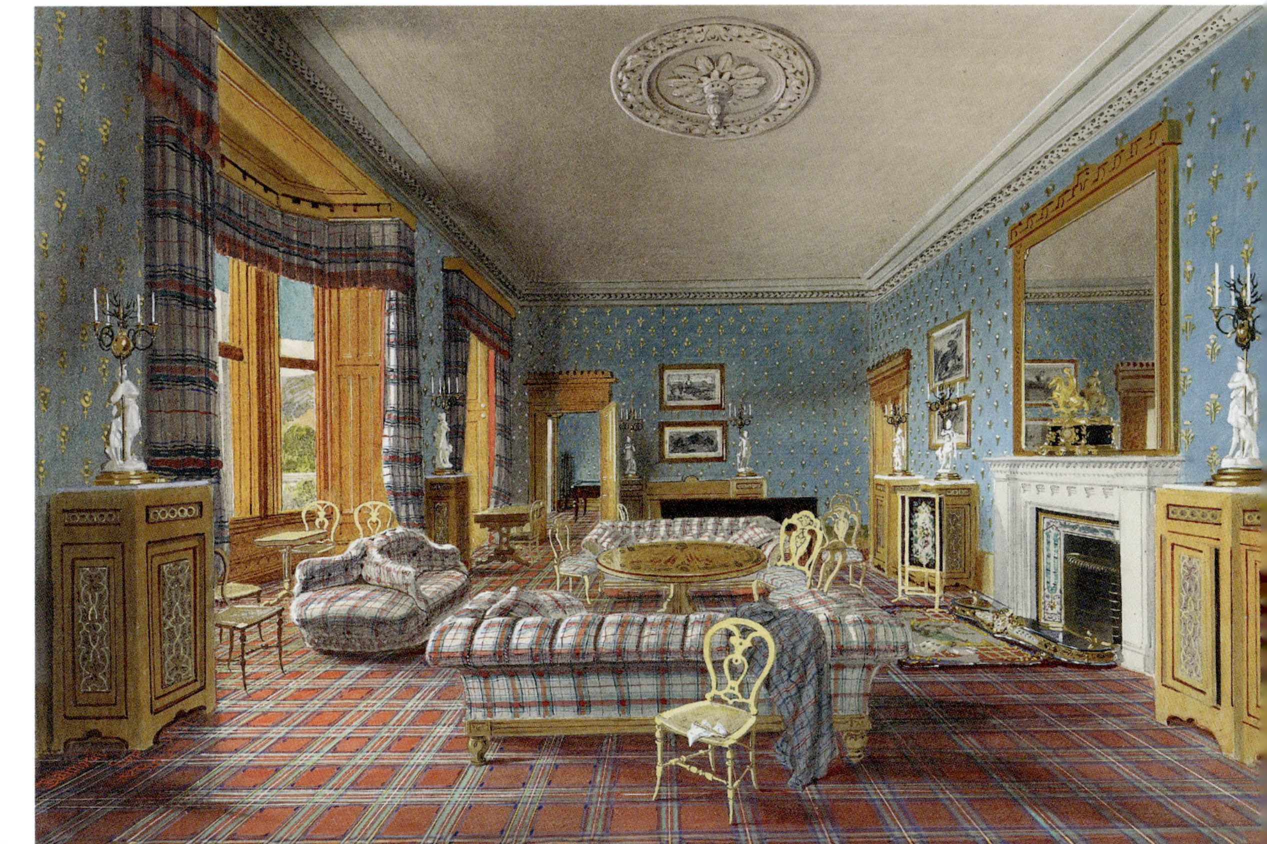

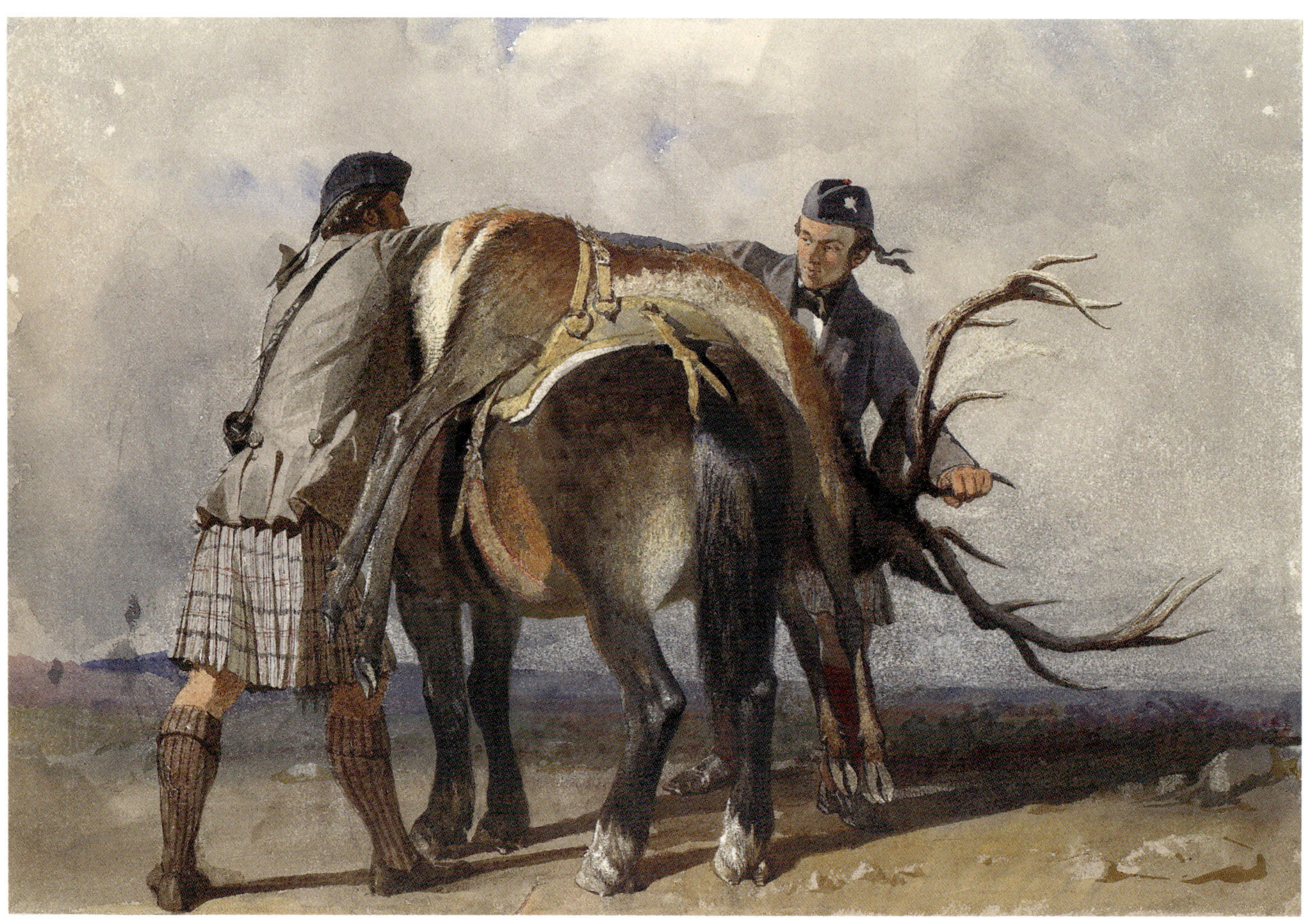



the dogs; the gillies and the pipers. Then the coming home – the Queen and her ladies going out to meet them, and the merry time afterwards; the torch-light sword-dancers on the green, and the servants' ball closing the day.'

Supporting all this was a staff of rugged, heavy-drinking Highlanders whom the Queen idealised as 'so good & so simple – & uncivilised, tho' well educated'. These sentiments, combined with her genuine interest in their lives and culture, pervade *Leaves from the Journal of Our Life in the Highlands*, the publishing sensation of 1868. Some thought the memoir would damage the Queen's regal image by dwelling too much on her servants and ordinary life, but it was widely translated and reprinted and, in 1884, followed by a second volume dedicated to her 'Loyal Highlanders'.

After Albert's death, 'this dear Paradise', scene of their happiest days, became the Queen's solace. She now spent nearly a third of the year at Balmoral, greatly to the inconvenience of her ministers. Until the late 1860s, several years after the opening of the Ballater section of the Deeside Railway, her daily despatch boxes still travelled from London to Perth and then 60 miles by pony and trap over the Cairnwell Pass, ascending 2,200 feet, often

*below* Balmoral stalkers photographed on 3 September 1853 by Prince Albert's librarian and tutor to the young princes, Dr Ernst Becker. Under Becker's influence, Victoria and Albert became early patrons and collectors of photography and led the way in documenting their lives through photographs.

through drifting snow. Many summoned to the castle dreaded the chilly rooms, the stodgy food and stultifying routine. From her thickly carpeted apartments smelling of orange-flower water, the Queen fixedly followed state business and micro-managed the domestic and outdoor arrangements; everything associated with Albert remained unchanged. Dutifully, she attended local events and entertained officials and her growing family of European royalty, but in later years her diminutive, black-clad figure was rarely seen, except when she ventured out for her daily rides.

For all the gloom of those final decades, Balmoral crystallised a version of Scottishness that shaped the social and cultural identity of Victorian Scotland. As the Royal Family's Scottish home, it exemplified a particular blend of 'unionist-nationalism', but it was not intended to make a political statement. In essence, Balmoral was the manifestation of a love affair between Victoria and Albert and the Highlands.

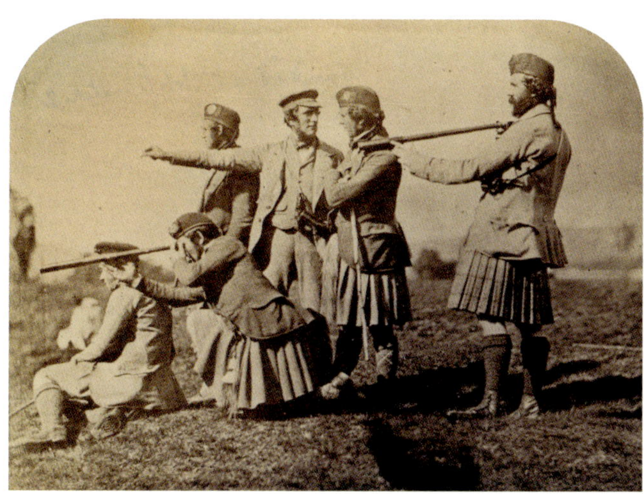

*right* 'Walks' for the stout monarch in her later years (she was less than five feet tall) generally meant being led miles on a pony by her personal servant John Brown, as depicted here by Charles Burton Barber on 26 August 1876. Brown epitomised the Queen's ideal of the 'shrewd, clever, noble' Highlander and become her 'omnipotent factotum' and close companion after Albert's death. She gave him this painting.

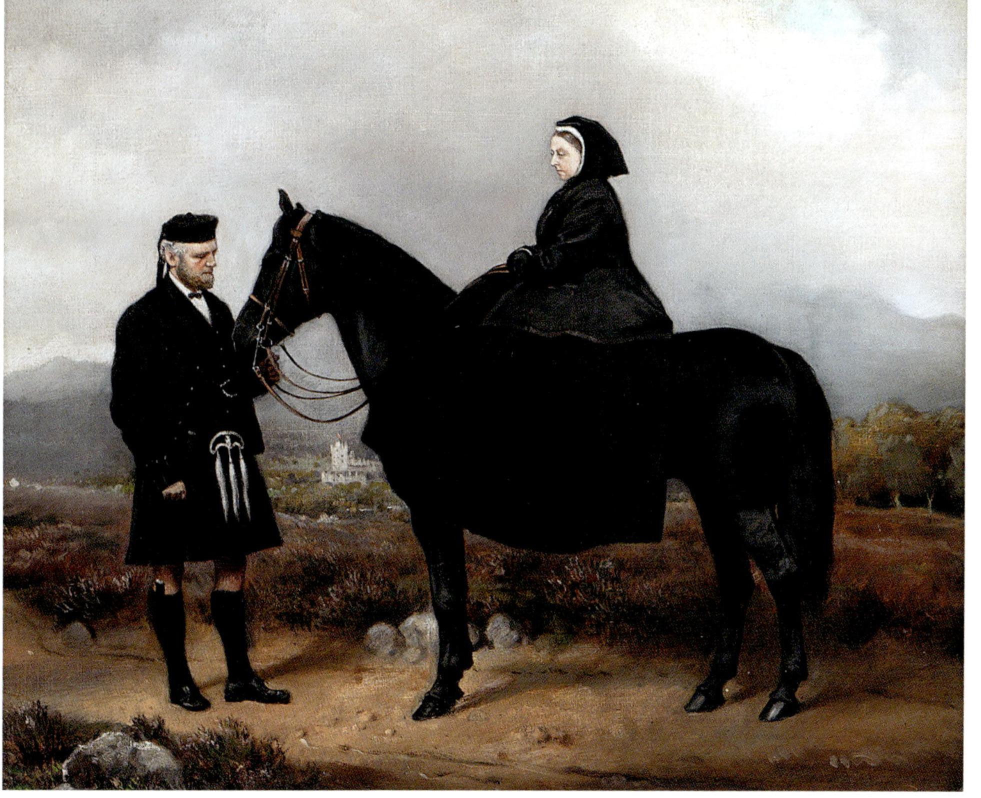

# The Twentieth Century: a Royal Retreat

On 6 November 1900, Queen Victoria visited her gamekeeper and then had lunch in Prince Albert's sitting room. Family deaths and illnesses, her own failing health and eyesight, and the general down-at-heel state of the castle, with its off-hand footmen reeking of whisky and abysmal food, exacerbated the gloom. It was to be her last day at Balmoral. She died at Osborne on 22 January 1901, and joined Albert in the mausoleum at Frogmore, a sprig of heather placed under the pillow in her coffin.

Edward VII preferred Sandringham to Balmoral, but he recognised the political importance of keeping a Scottish residence and entered into the Highland spirit when he visited each autumn. He had grown up with kilts and pipers and embraced this aspect, while dutifully attending Royal fixtures, such as the Braemar Gathering, services at Crathie Kirk and the presentation of regimental colours. But he was appalled by the amount of alcohol consumed on the estate and made drastic cuts to stalkers' whisky rations, banning drunkenness with severe penalties.

A contemporary report outlined the King's resolve to 'give greater comfort and convenience without destroying the air of simplicity, almost of homeliness, which has always been the distinguishing feature of Royalty's Highland dwelling place'. The entrance hall was duly remodelled, the servants' wing extended and other improvements made, for which the prominent Edinburgh architect and restorer of medieval abbeys, Robert Rowand Anderson, received a knighthood in 1902.

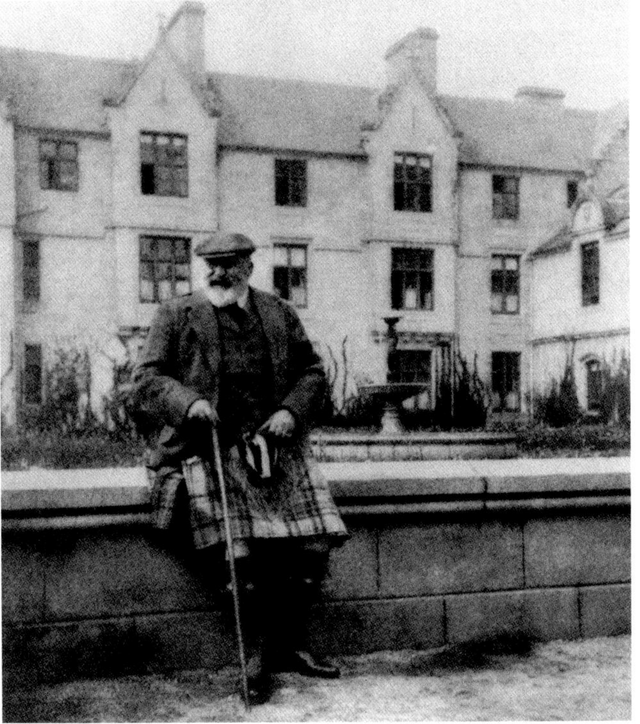

*left* Edward VII wearing a mourning armband, sitting in front of the Tower Garden at Balmoral. Queen Alexandra took the photograph around 1906 and included it in her personal copy of her *Christmas Gift Book*, which was published in 1908 to raise funds for charity.

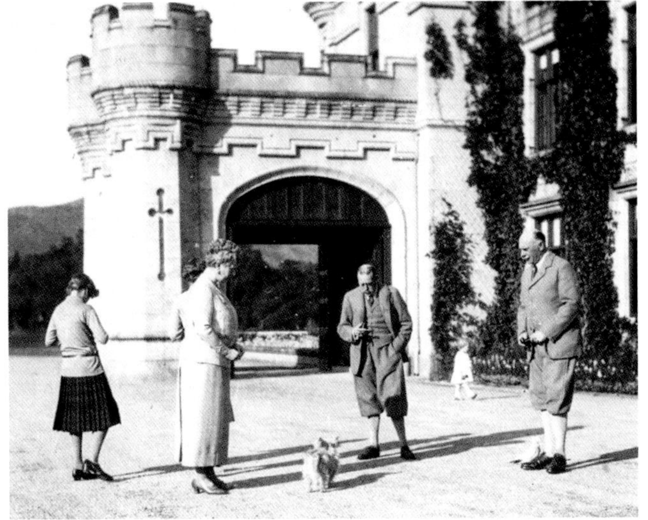

*below left* Queen Mary and King George V with their cairn terrier Snip, flanked by an unidentified kilted figure [left] and the Earl of Athlone [right] in September 1928. The toddler in the background is the future Elizabeth II.

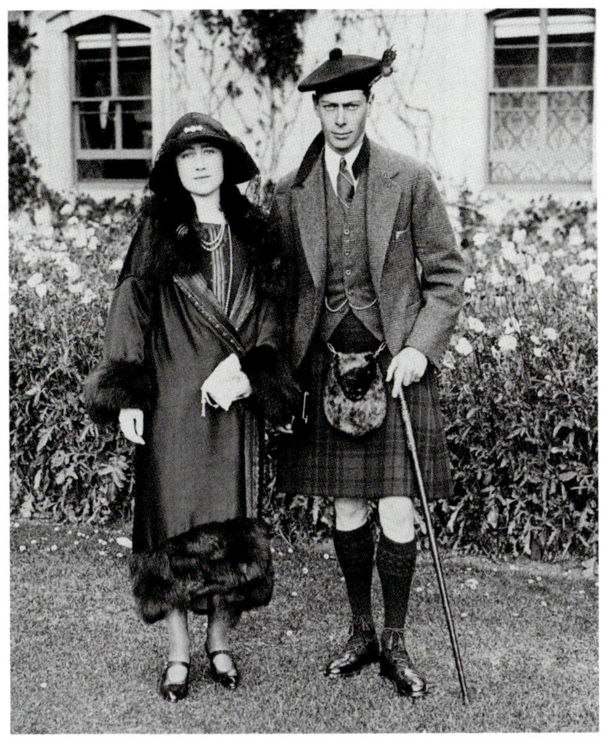

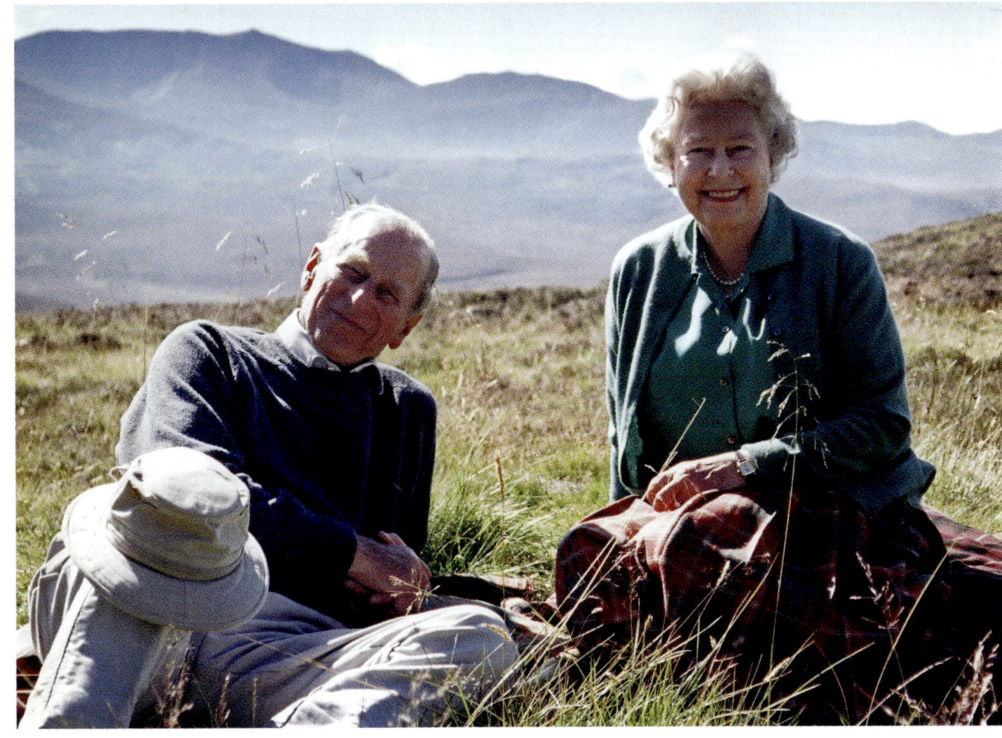



For Queen Alexandra, Balmoral unleashed a new-found pleasure in the Highlands, yet she could never escape the late Queen's presence. 'One misses her at every step and corner and it seems almost like sacrilege sitting here writing at *her* table,' she confided; she would leave all the treasures untouched. She did, however, replace the drawing-room tartan with something more restrained.

Love of the Highland landscape and outdoor pursuits is a running thread that links the regimes of six monarchs at Balmoral. 'I am never so happy as when I am fishing the pools of the Dee, with a long day before me,' wrote George V, who, like his grandmother, had an easy rapport with the tenantry and took a keen interest in piping. In the 1920s, aspects of life here became simpler – 'The Queen knits of an evening … we go to bed early,' a guest recalled – although the tradition of picnics transported by Daimler and served by liveried footmen continued.

Belying her biographer's assertion that she was 'a decidedly urban queen with little enthusiasm for Scotland', Queen Mary developed the gardens at Balmoral and appears in photographs enjoying expeditions on Loch Muick. In the castle, she applied her deep knowledge of the Royal Collections to rearranging the rooms and pictures.

George VI had a visceral attachment to the Highlands and knew all the flora, fauna and topography. As a young man in 1919, he established annual summer camps for teenage boys and he would later lead expeditions into the hills. He introduced a more personal style of estate management at Balmoral and, with his Scottish wife, created a less formal atmosphere for close-knit family holidays. After his death, the widowed

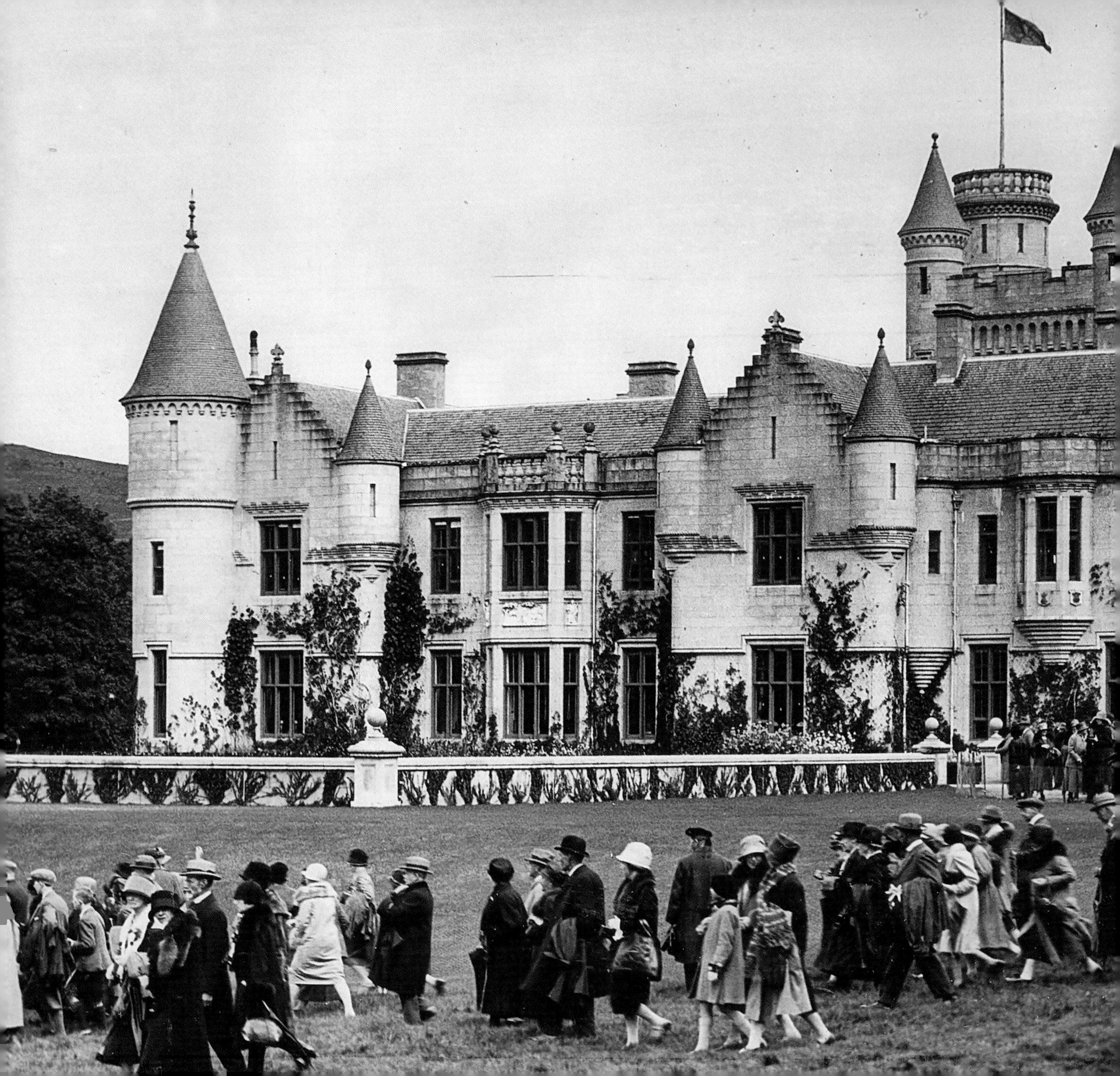

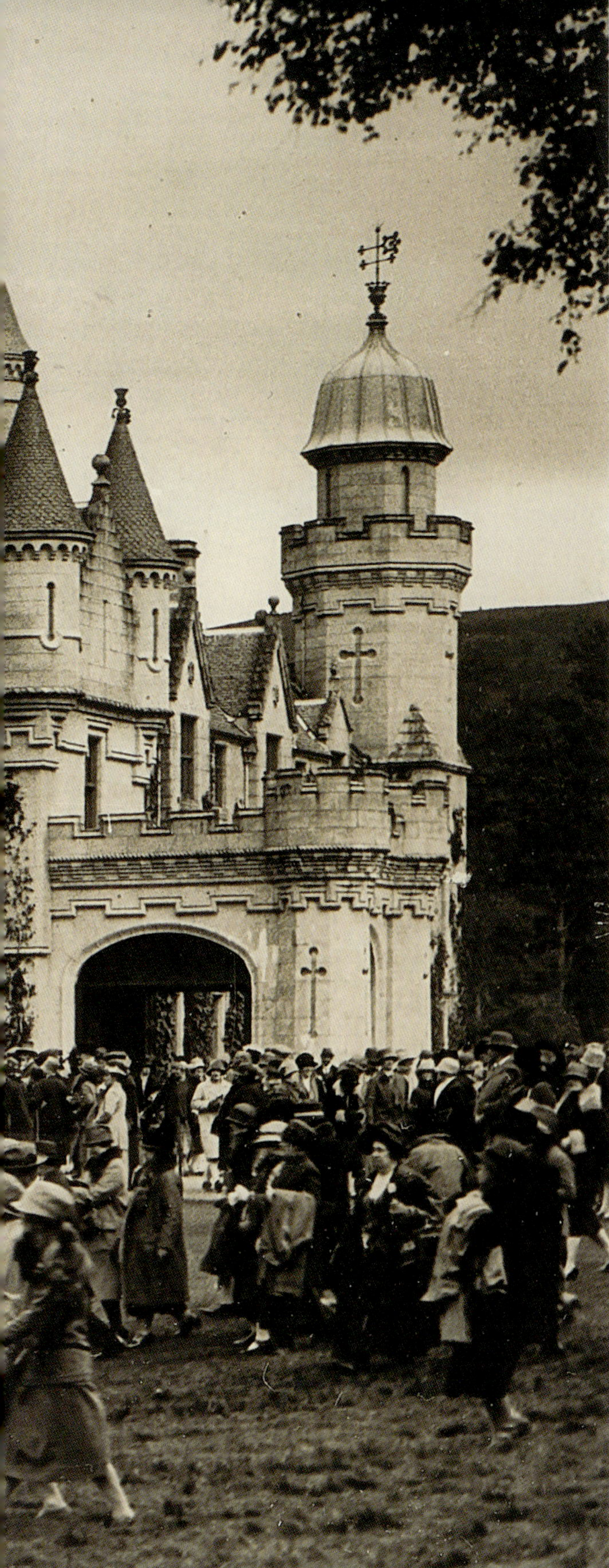



Queen Elizabeth established her Deeside home at Birkhall, a Georgian laird's house with land in Glenmuick that had become part of the estate in 1885 and is now Their Majesties' private home.

During her long reign, Elizabeth II reaffirmed Balmoral's image as the Royal Family's beloved Highland retreat. A true countrywoman, she spent every August to October at Balmoral and was never happier than when out on the hill in all weathers. With the Duke of Edinburgh, who oversaw the running of the estate, she became closely involved in breeding livestock, establishing the Balmoral Fold of Highland cattle and the pony stud. Despite the explosion of tourism on Deeside, precipitating the development of visitor facilities and wider public access to the grounds, she could be relatively free here and interact more naturally with the local people.

Physically, the castle had changed little when she inherited it in 1952. She augmented the picture hang, de-tartaned and re-decorated, but largely it remained as it was and continues to be used in the way that was intended. In its dual role as an extension to Court and the sovereign's private Scottish home, Balmoral represents a significant part of the Royal Family's identity, a part that the late Queen did much to shape. It is fitting that it was here, on 8 September 2022, that Britain's longest-reigning monarch died, for Balmoral was always her favourite home.

# Balmoral: a New Era

When he inherited Balmoral in 2022, The King, supported by The Queen, initiated a series of transformative projects that have seen the castle interiors revitalised and opened to the public for the first time and the gardens redeveloped. Like Prince Albert, who played such a central role in the design and orientation of the castle and its buildings, His Majesty has a deep interest in architecture and the arts and a great love of the outdoors. He understands that the essence of Balmoral is its relationship to the landscape and this is something that comes across in many of his improvements, which he oversees with a meticulous eye.

The reception rooms, arranged in L-plan around the west and north wings, and the Royal apartments above, drink in the views through large windows and feel light and airy. Inevitably, however, their distinctive character had become diluted over the years. Now, with interior designer Annabel Elliot and curators from the Royal Collection helping to enable his vision, The King has injected pattern and colour back into the furnishings and added many objects of aesthetic and historical interest. He has also rearranged the paintings in a denser hang and given more emphasis to the fine collection of Landseers that he particularly admires.

For all the Prime Ministers and other prestigious visitors entertained here during Court, the overriding impression of these rooms is that of a comfortable home for informal gatherings of family and friends.

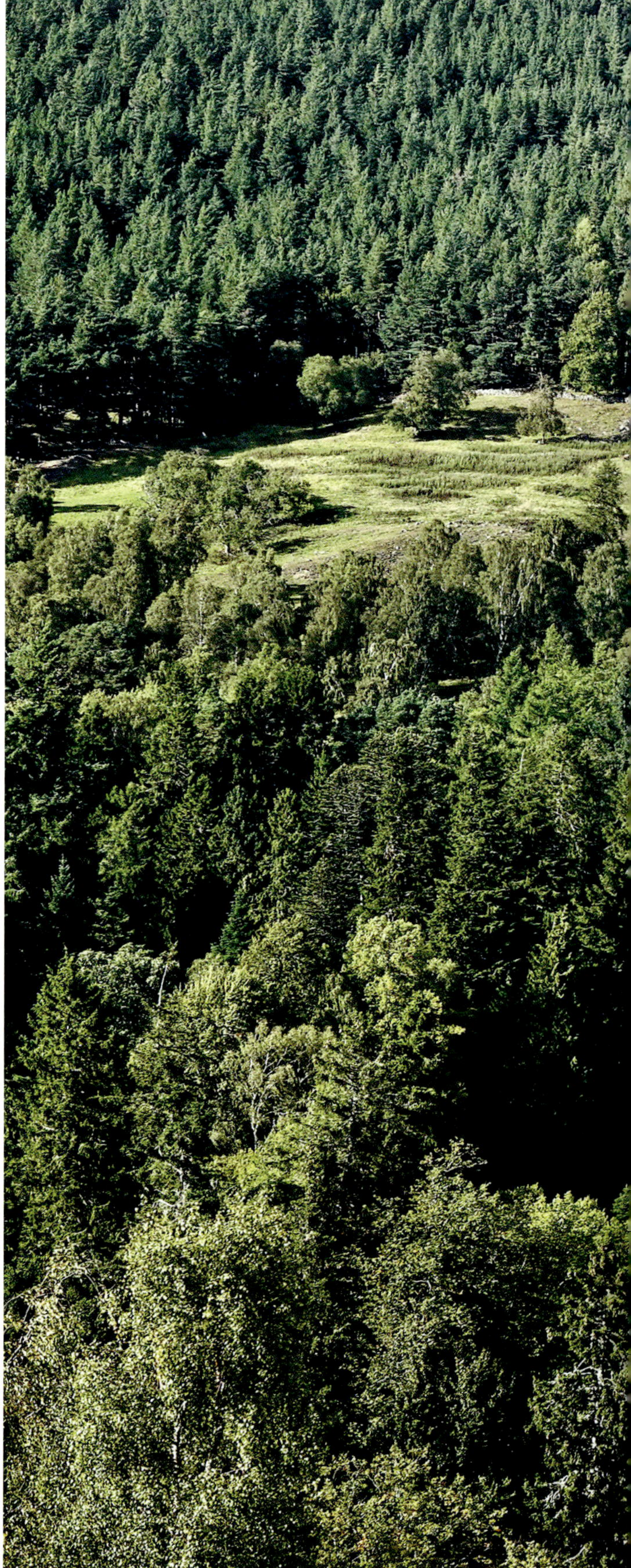

*right* Built of silvery-grey Invergelder granite, the castle stands out against wooded Creag Mhòr. This is the south front, with the entrance on the far left, flanked by the visitors' wing, which includes the prime-ministerial suite. A lower range links the main quadrangle to the great tower, which contains the Equerries' Room and wine cellars, with staff rooms and the clocktower store above. Beyond the tower, the service court adopts a more Scots-vernacular vein.

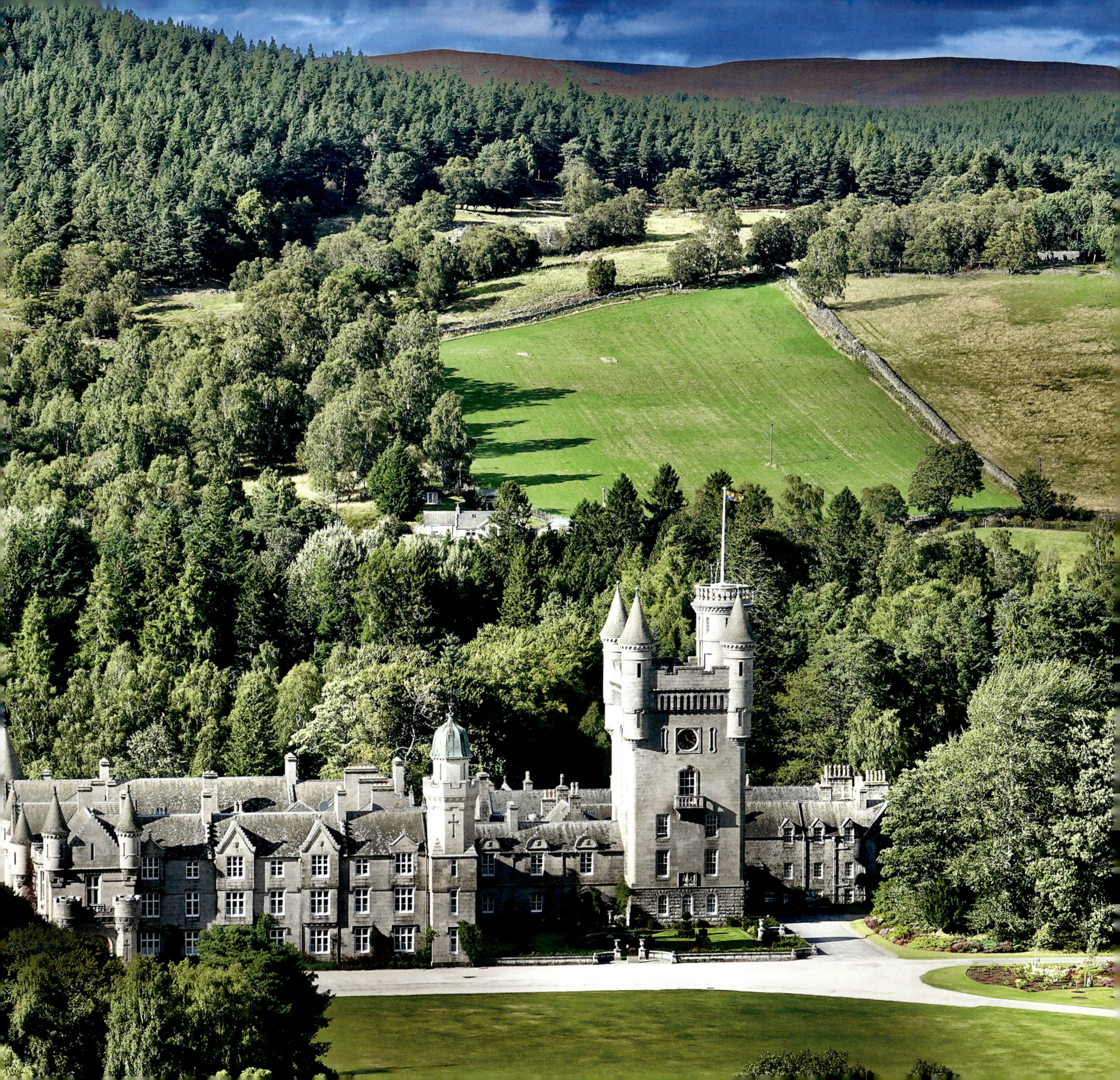

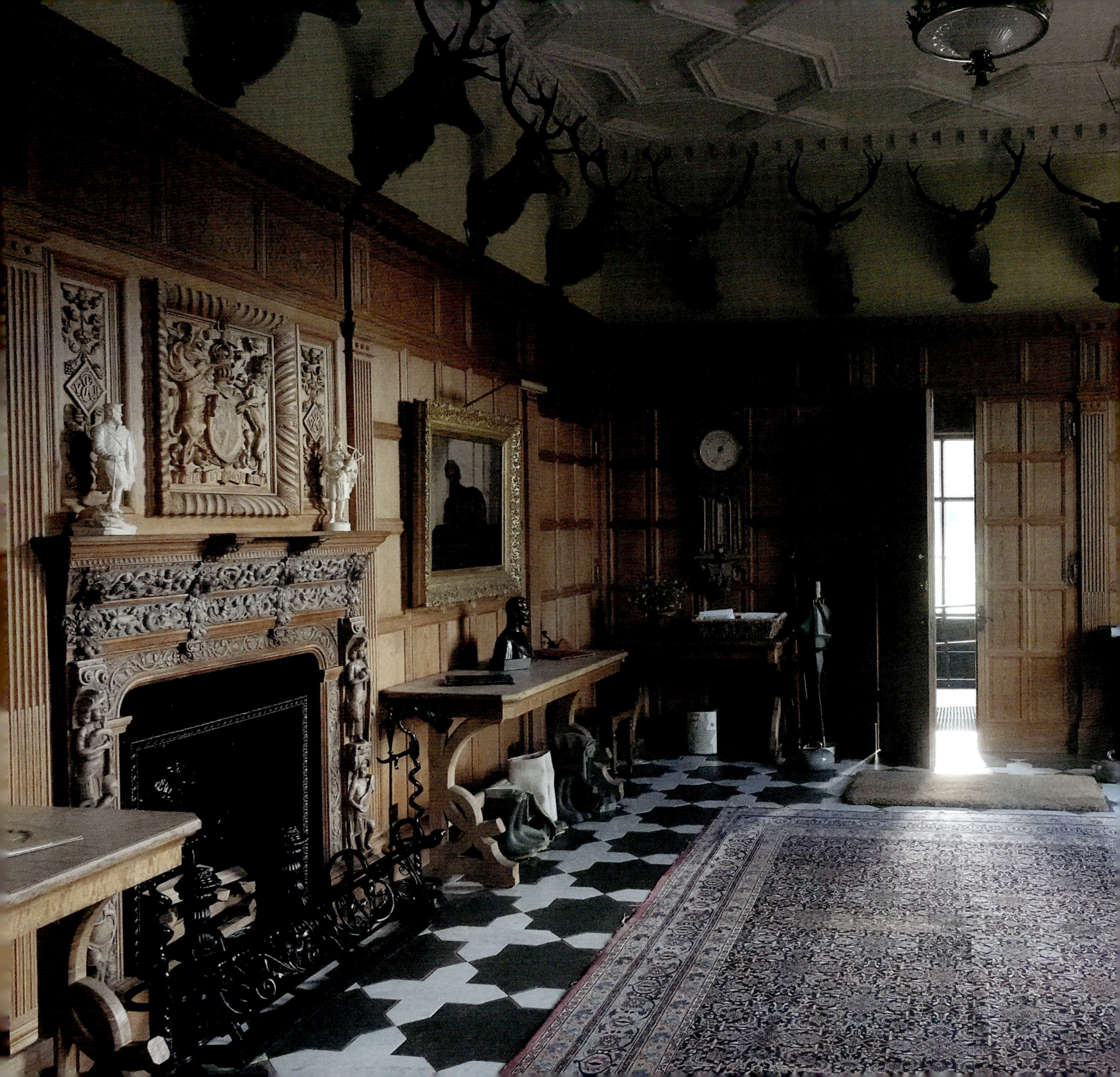

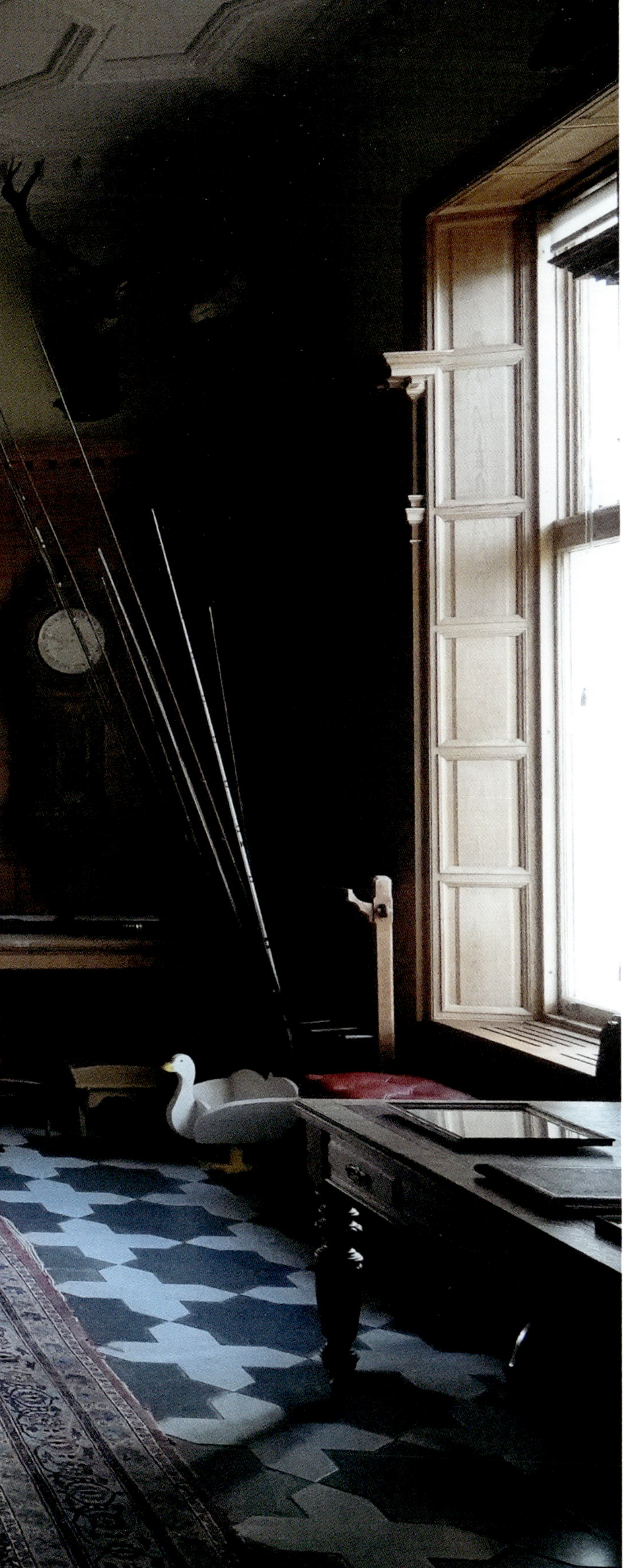



# The Entrance Hall

The first impression on entering Balmoral from the fort-like porte-cochère is the relatively modest scale and informal character of the entrance hall. In its original form, the room was starkly furnished and painted to simulate large blocks of marble, with stag heads, deerskin rugs and an antler and thistle chandelier emphasising the out-of-doors feel. Despite references to Prince Albert's cosmopolitan taste in the quality of furnishings and swish inlaid marble floor, it emulated a genre of rustic hunting-hall style shooting lodges, with a nod to the antiquarian displays popularised by Sir Walter Scott at Abbotsford. The central niche was dominated from 1861 by a full-height bronze statue of the 11th-century Scottish king, Malcolm Canmore, and the chimneypiece had been rescued from old Balmoral. Dating from the 1830s remodelling of that house, this Jacobean-style relic was almost certainly made by the firm of the leading Edinburgh cabinet maker, William Trotter, whose design volumes include references to Balmoral. Trotter often replicated old carved timberwork or made pieces by framing up antique fragments.

Edward VII found the room cold and austere and had it lined with Ballochbuie Scots pine in 1901–03 (it was stripped and lightened by Queen Mary after 1910). The panelling fulfils the Jacobean theme set by the chimneypiece and ceiling, with skilfully articulated pilaster strips, carved cabochon decoration and a Royal Arms overmantel redolent of Craigievar or Glamis. The architect Robert Rowand Anderson, who carried out other work at Balmoral around this time,

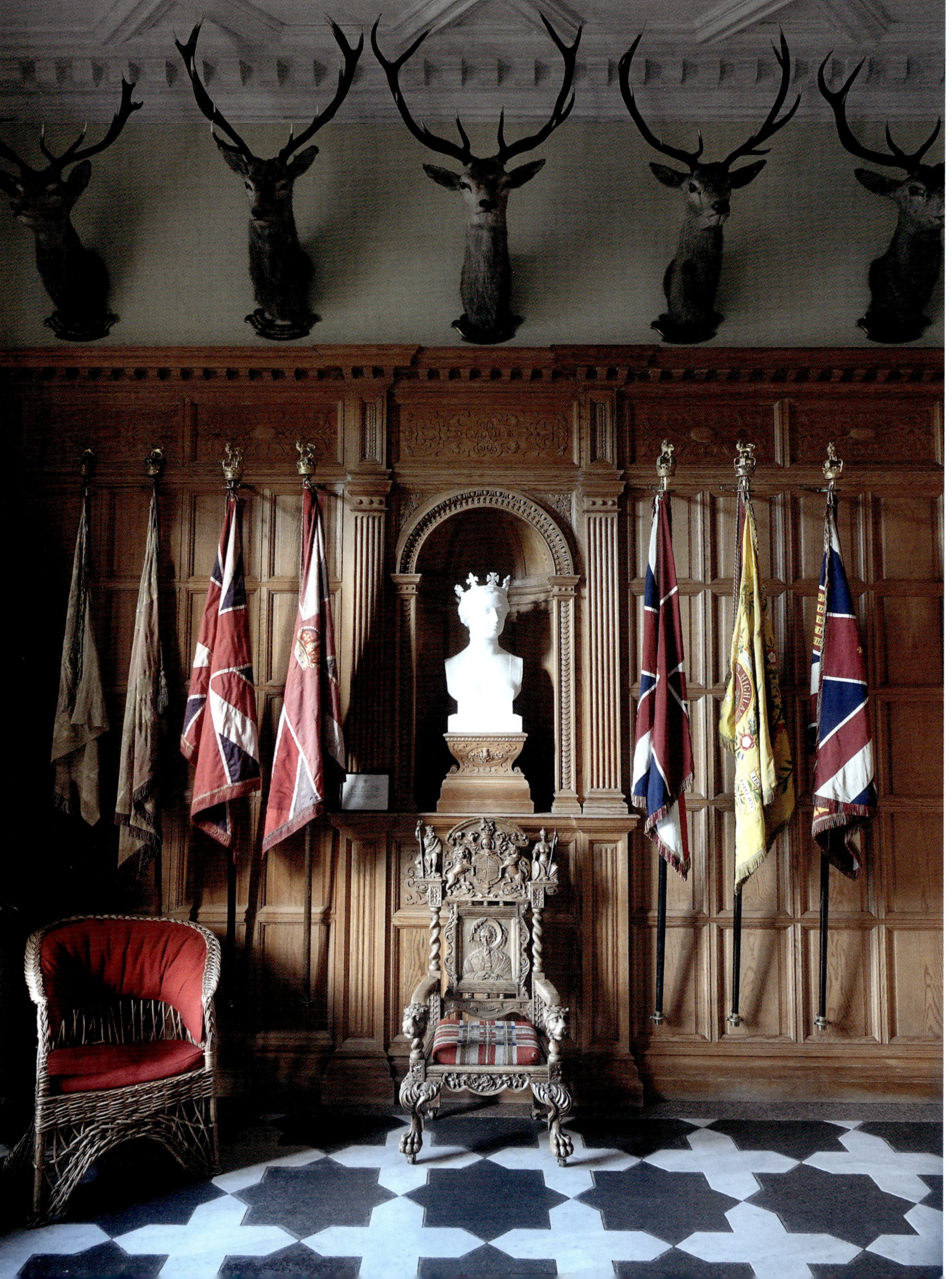

*left*  Queen Victoria in her Diamond Diadem presides over the hall above an armchair made in 1875–99 from oak salvaged from Chester Cathedral. They are framed by Colours of the 79th Regiment of Foot, the Cameron Highlanders, which were carried throughout the Crimean War and the Indian Mutiny. They were at the fall of Sebastopol in 1855, news of which reached the Queen three days after she moved into the new castle. A bonfire was lit on Craigowan and there was much whisky-fuelled cheering and dancing.

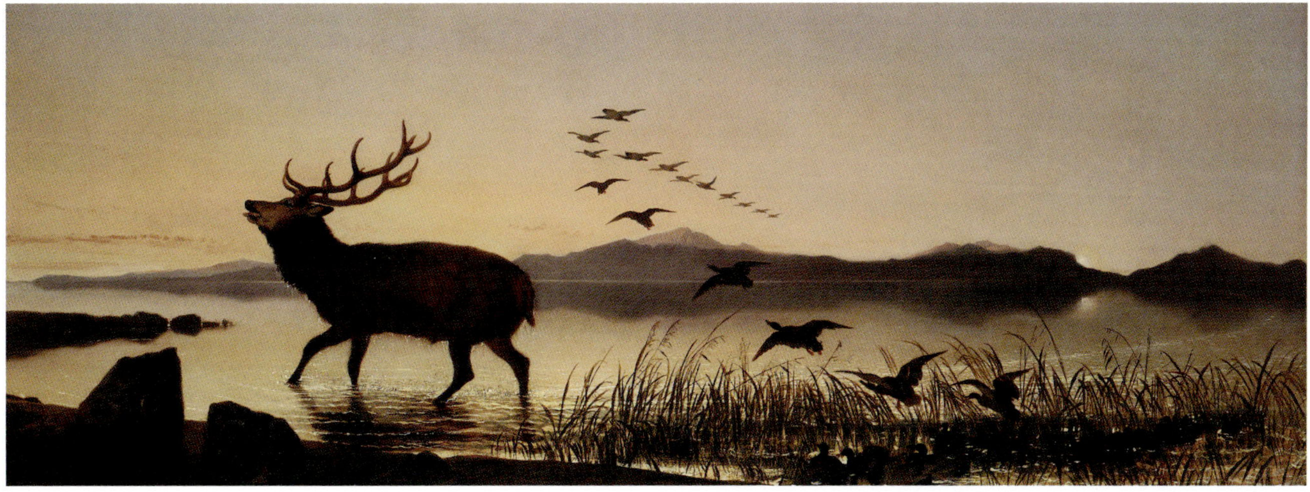



*right* Landseer's *The Sanctuary* shows Loch Maree, where the stag has swum to an island to escape the hunt. The finest of several paintings by the artist that have been brought together in the entrance hall, it caught Queen Victoria's eye when it was exhibited at the Royal Academy in 1842. It originally hung in Prince Albert's writing room at Windsor.

*below right* William Theed's 1860 bronze and gilt figure depicts Malcolm III – Malcolm Canmore – who ruled Scotland from 1058 to 1093, invaded England five times and killed Macbeth in 1057. Queen Victoria commissioned William Theed to make it for Albert for Christmas in 1860; it was to be her last gift to him. It occupied the central niche until the room was panelled in the early 1900s.

is credited with the design. The use of friezes reflects that in contemporary Aesthetic interiors, as does the artistic high fender, but the overall tone is historicist and very different to the rooms it precedes. Efforts were made to reinstate some of the former objects, such as the elaborately cased barometer and perpetual calendar that had previously flanked the fireplace.

The focus on entering is the niche containing Alexander and William Brodie's marble bust of Queen Victoria (1867), which Edward VII moved to this central position when he remodelled the room. His Majesty's recent introduction of more furniture, paintings and objects, together with a carpet to add colour and texture, has made the hall feel more homely and welcoming. The presence of Tsar Nicholas II, who visited Balmoral in 1896, adds a fascinating historical layer in the form of Pietro Canonica's bust of 1910, while the casual array of fishing rods, gumboots, umbrellas and curling stones reminds us that the house we have just entered was built for outdoor holidays and still functions that way today.

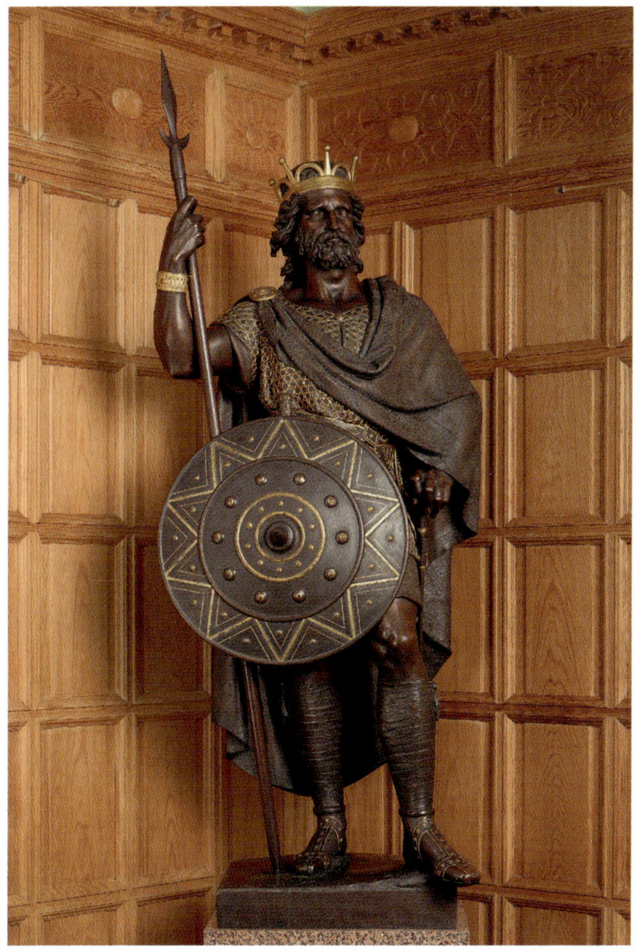

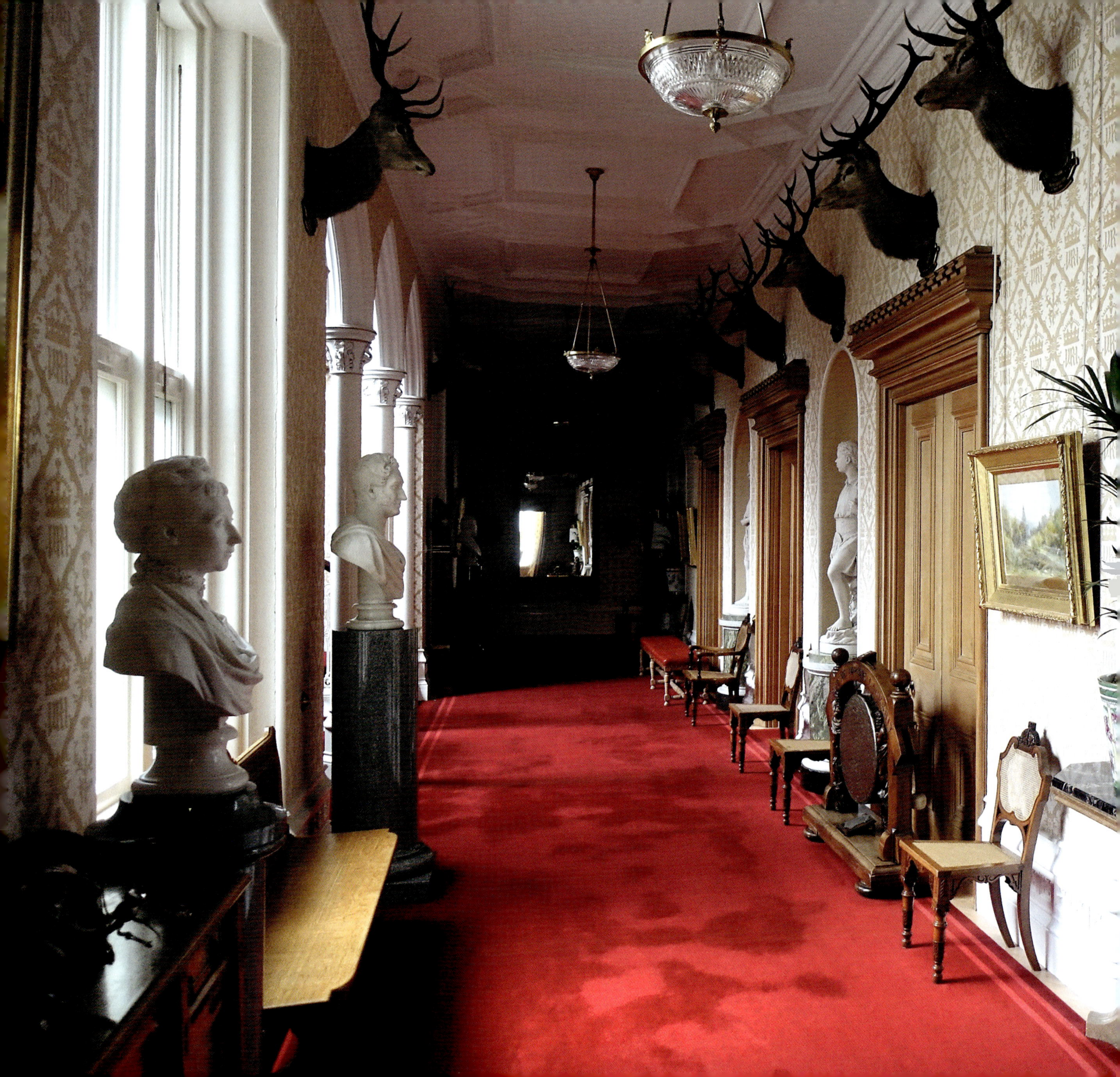

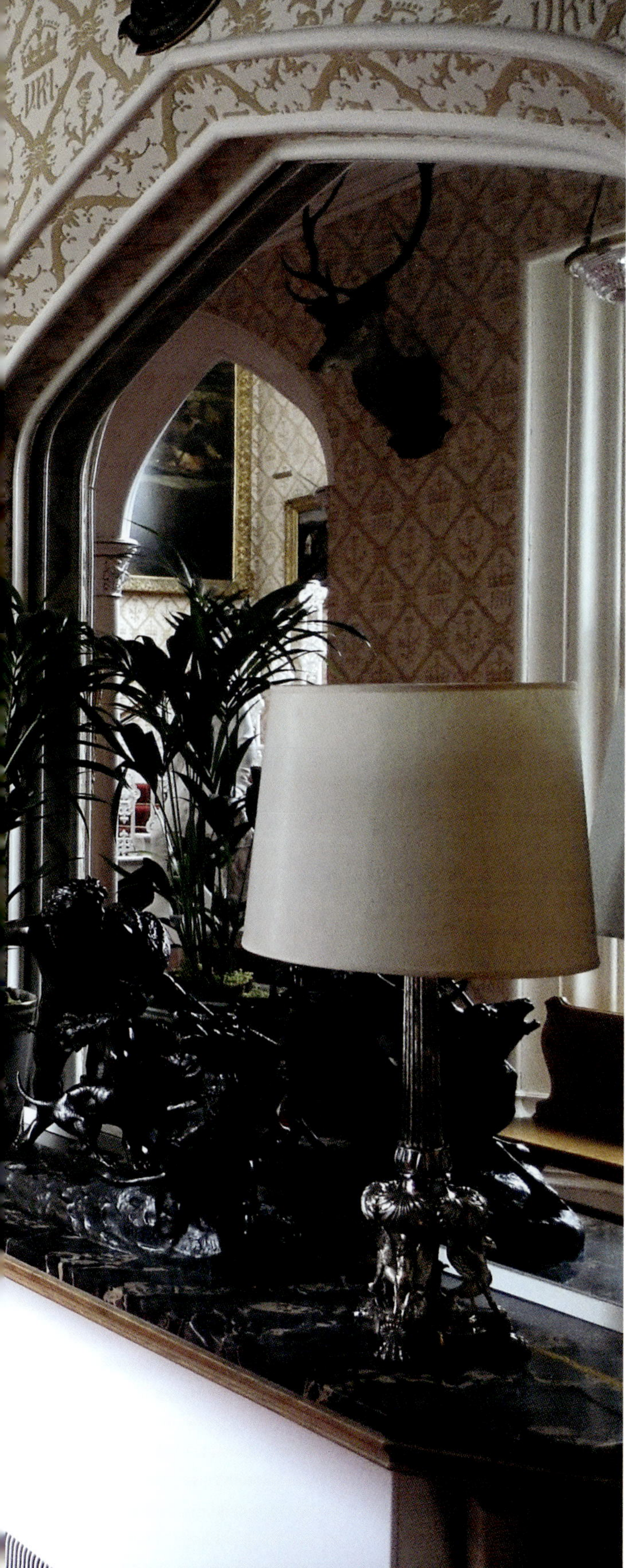



# The Red Corridor

The principal suite of interconnecting rooms is ranged along two sides of a quadrangle, served by corridors around the inner courtyard. The Red Corridor is the main arterial route, providing access through finely moulded doorcases to the rooms along the west range. The main staircase opens off it through a Gothic arcade and rises to the Royal landing, from which the private apartments are accessed.

Originally painted to imitate marble, the circulation spaces were redecorated with flock wallpaper designed by William Morris for Queen Victoria's Golden Jubilee in 1887. Taxidermy at Balmoral was limited to the hall and corridors, with antlers on ornate mounts crowning the stairwell. After Albert's death, the Queen ordered that none of his hunting trophies be moved and no additions made to the corridors.

Victoria and Albert kept their sculpture and paintings (even Highland-themed ones) down at Osborne and Windsor, which explains a contemporary description of the corridor as filled with 'stuffed birds and rare kinds of stones found here'. Since then, it has become more of a sculpture gallery. The niches flanking the drawing-room door contain marble statues of Prince Albert Victor and Prince George (later George v), commissioned in 1875 from Francis John Williamson. The King was keen to enhance the historic and family interest of the public tour and has added several busts brought up from Windsor, so that four generations are now represented.

# The Dining Room

With its buffet recess framed by pilasters, modillion cornice and dummy door for symmetry, the dining room conforms to the restrained neo-Classical style of Balmoral's interiors, within which its chimneypiece, cut from Peterhead granite, and Holland & Sons oak furniture sustain Smith's Tudor-Gothic theme. Complemented by the studded, red-leather dining chairs, the sideboards and side tables suggest the influence of A. W. N. Pugin, for whom the firm had made furniture for Westminster Palace.

The walls were originally hung with prints, but six portraits of Victoria, Albert and their children, painted by the German portraitist Franz Xavier Winterhalter, now lend colour and vitality to a room that has lost its original palette of vibrant green and red. Particular favourites of the Queen were the pair flanking the fireplace, which Albert gave to her as birthday presents.

The Prince's artistic input at Balmoral extended to a number of decorative objects of a personal and overtly Scottish nature. The Atholl Inkstand, which he designed and had made by the jeweller John Wornell and other craftsmen, is an outstanding example. Studded with stones collected on walks and the teeth of stags he'd shot, it reflects his sentimental and decorative use of local materials. Stag teeth were particularly popular in jewellery, many examples of which Albert designed, having introduced the fashion from his native Thuringia, where the hunting culture was strong.

On a similar theme are the gilt-bronze candelabra commissioned for the dining room around

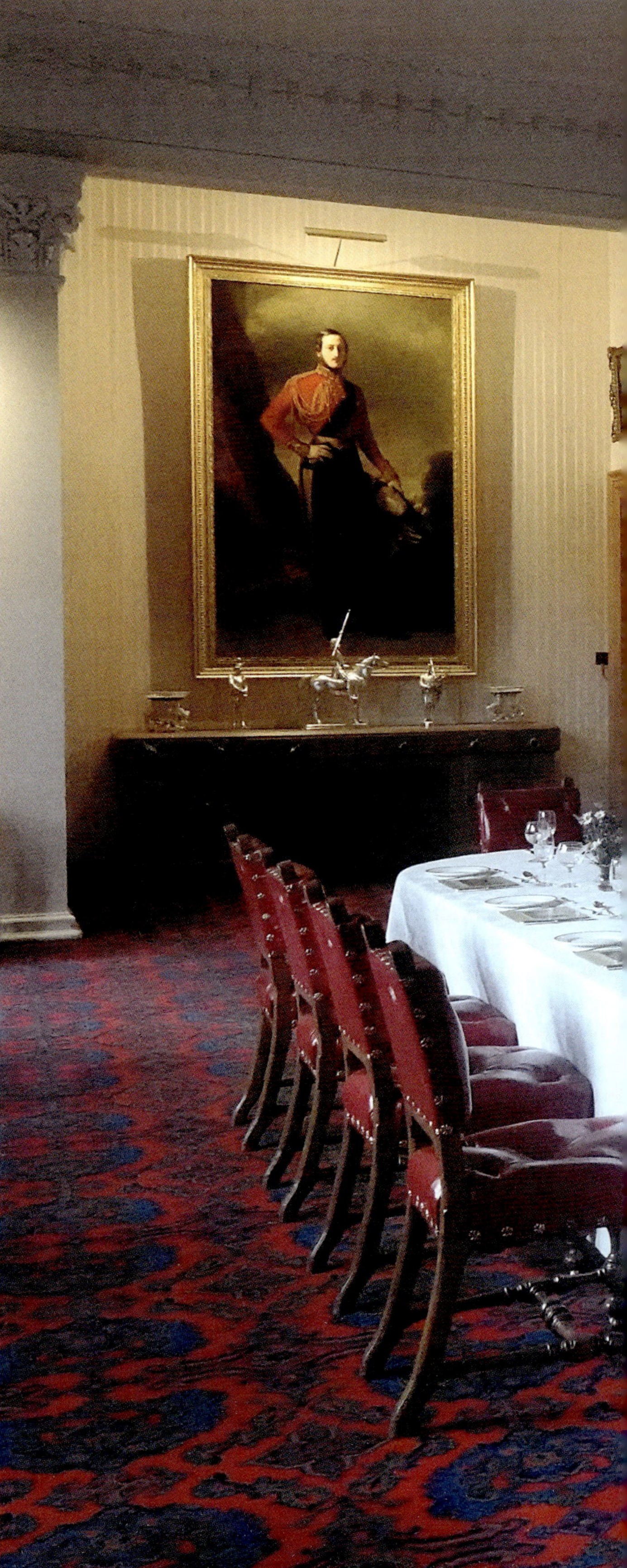

*right* Presiding over the dining room are Winterhalter's portraits of Queen Victoria and Prince Albert (1844–45), and their children. The charming group on the left of the fireplace (1856) shows Princess Louise with Princes Arthur and Leopold; on the right are Prince Alfred and Princess Helena (1848–49). The Minton dessert plates, decorated with dogs after Landseer, were commissioned for Balmoral in 1871. The silver statuettes are by Boehm and the Louis XIV mantel clock is after Boulle.

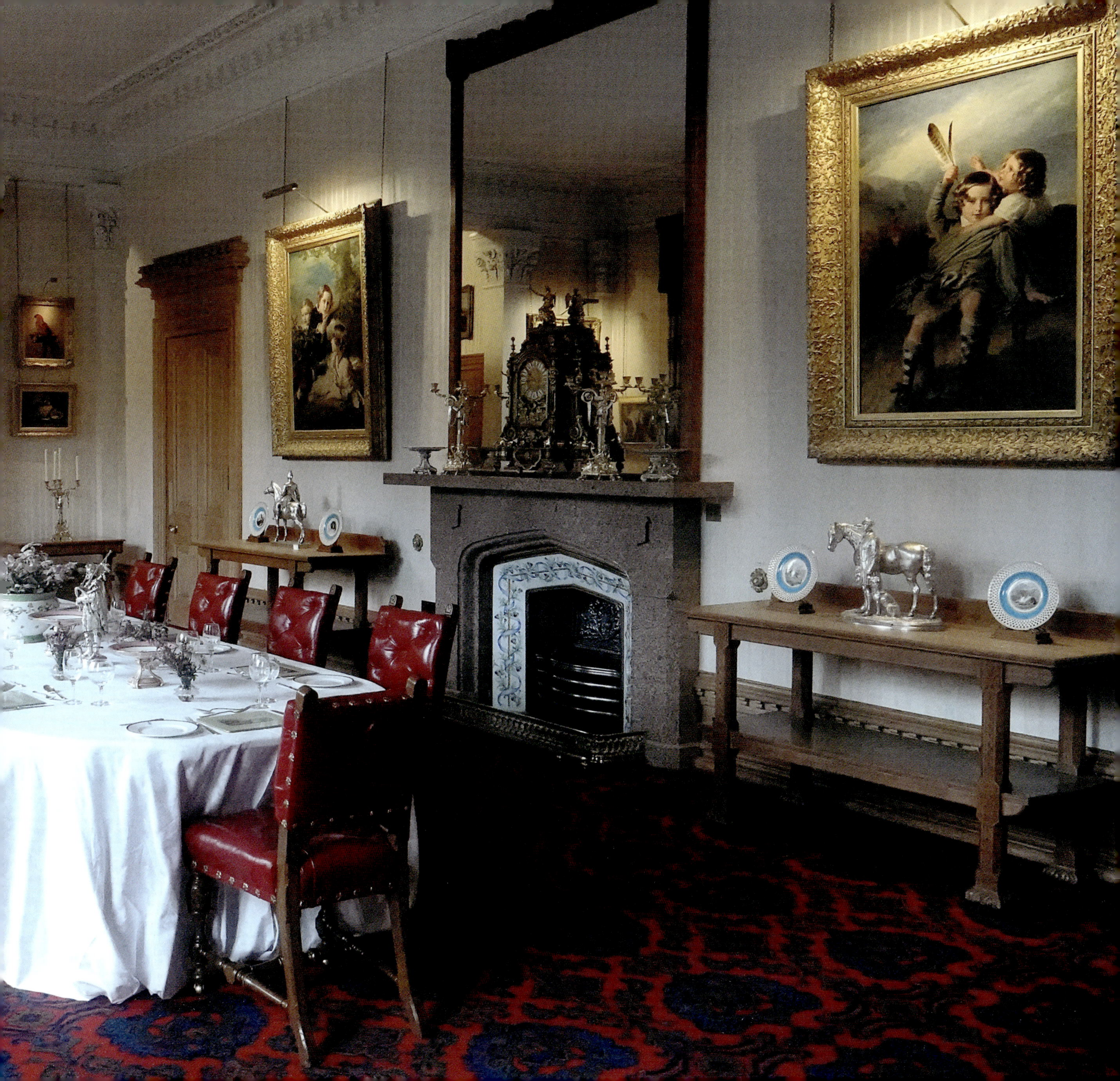

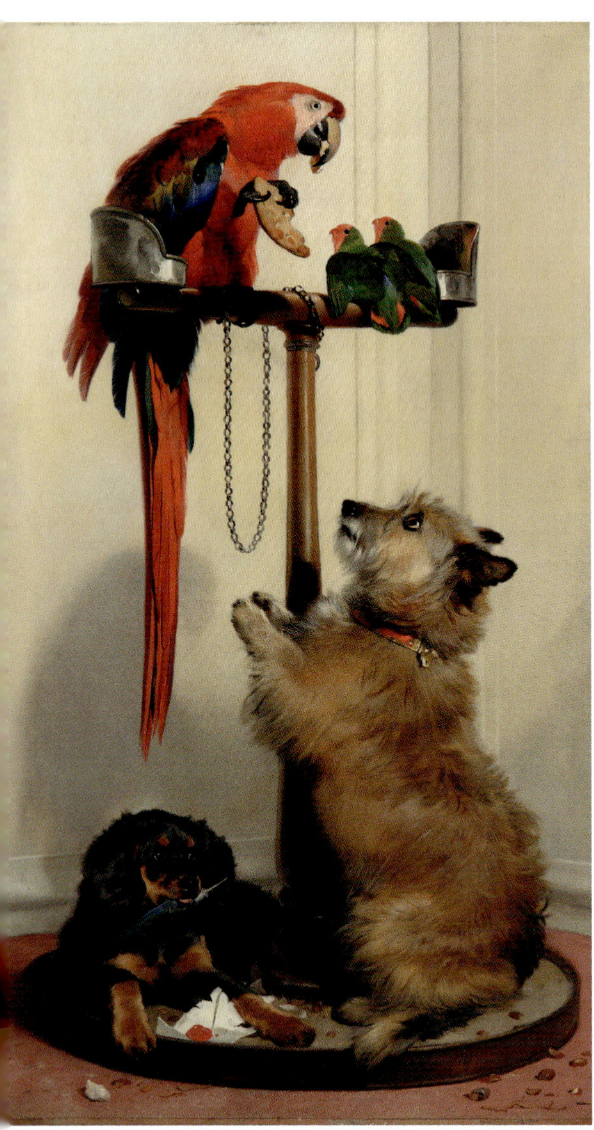

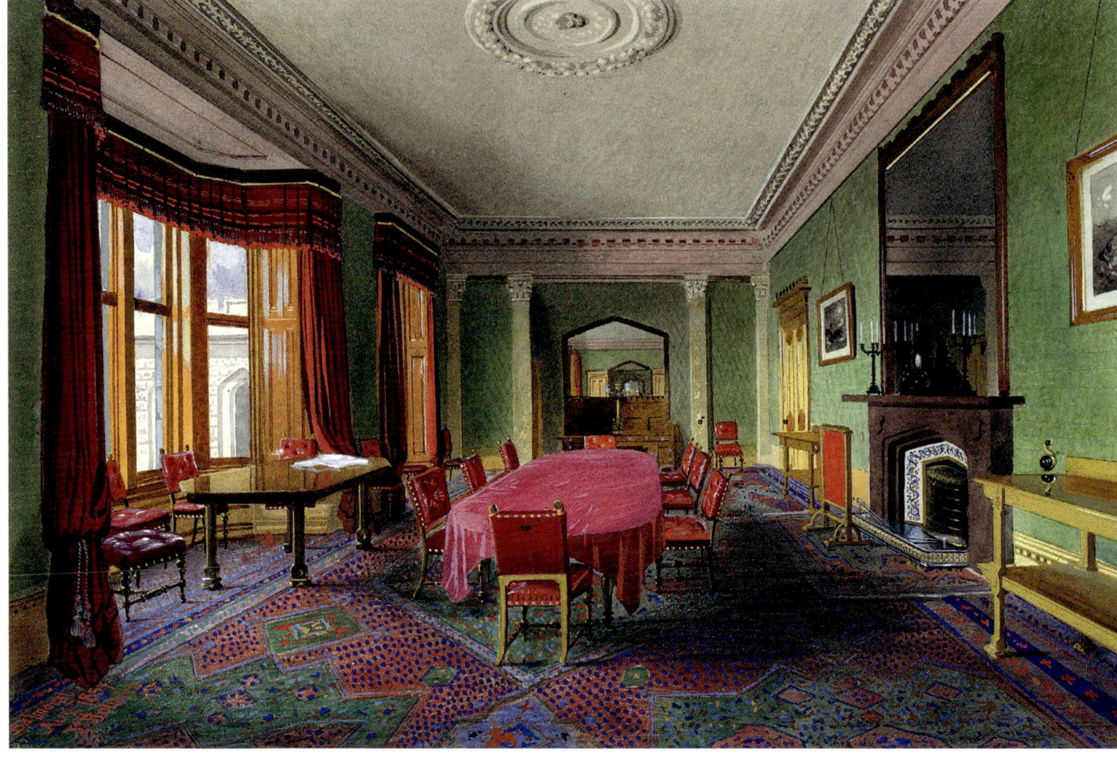

*left* The rugged Atholl Inkstand (1844–45) exemplifies Albert's love of connecting decorative objects physically to a place and includes two inscriptions commemorating the family's idyllic 1842 holiday in Atholl.

*above* James Roberts's 1857 watercolour shows the dining room's original rich palette, unpainted marble pilasters with gilt capitals and curtains described by Holland & Sons as 'fine Tartan cashmere lined with Merino and bound with a plaited valence trimmed with a fringe'. The 'best Turkey carpet' cost £58 2s and was similar to the one depicted by James Giles in his 1855 view of the dining room at old Balmoral Castle.

*above* Commissioned by Queen Victoria in 1839, Landseer's *Islay, Tilco, a Macaw and Two Lovebirds* shows her faithful Skye terrier Islay and Tilco, her Sussex spaniel. The element of humour is characteristic in Landseer's animal paintings – see also his painting of marmosets on a pineapple. Both works have recently joined two other Landseers in this room.

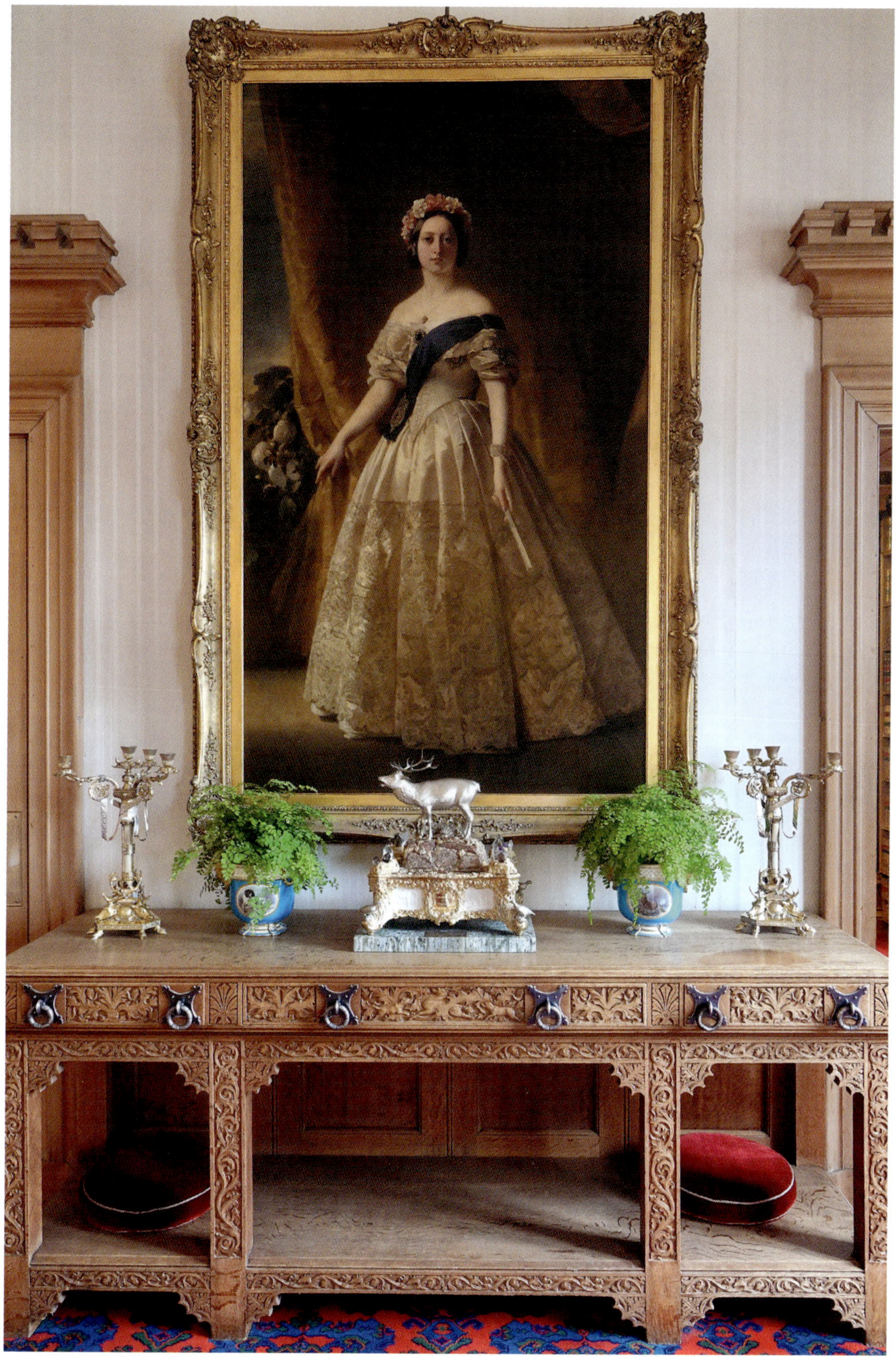

1855. Modelled by Pierre-Emile Jeannest and electro-plated by Elkingtons, each comprises a shaft of antler bone supporting branches with thistle candle holders, their scrolls draped with plaided silver ribbons. Stag heads with entwined antlers alternate with cairngorms around the base, which stands on hooves.

His Majesty has recently displayed more of his silver collection, notably Boehm's Highlander, athlete and equestrian statuettes that Queen Victoria so admired. The silverware adds greatly to the atmosphere of candlelit dinners, during which The King's Piper plays at intervals. Presidents and prime ministers, crowned heads and luminaries, friends and family have all been treated to this tradition, which was instituted by Victoria and Albert, who became 'quite fond of the bagpipes' while staying at Taymouth Castle. The piper also plays daily outside the castle at 9 a.m. Not all guests are enthusiastic, but happily there's no longer cause to complain, as did Lord Clarendon, that 'the Queen had the windows open while we were at dinner'.

*left* Winterhalter's 1845 portrait of Queen Victoria hangs over one of the Holland & Sons' sideboards, which originally had a mirrored back (removed by Edward VII). Flanking the Atholl Inkstand are two of the Highland-themed candelabra commissioned for the room in 1855.

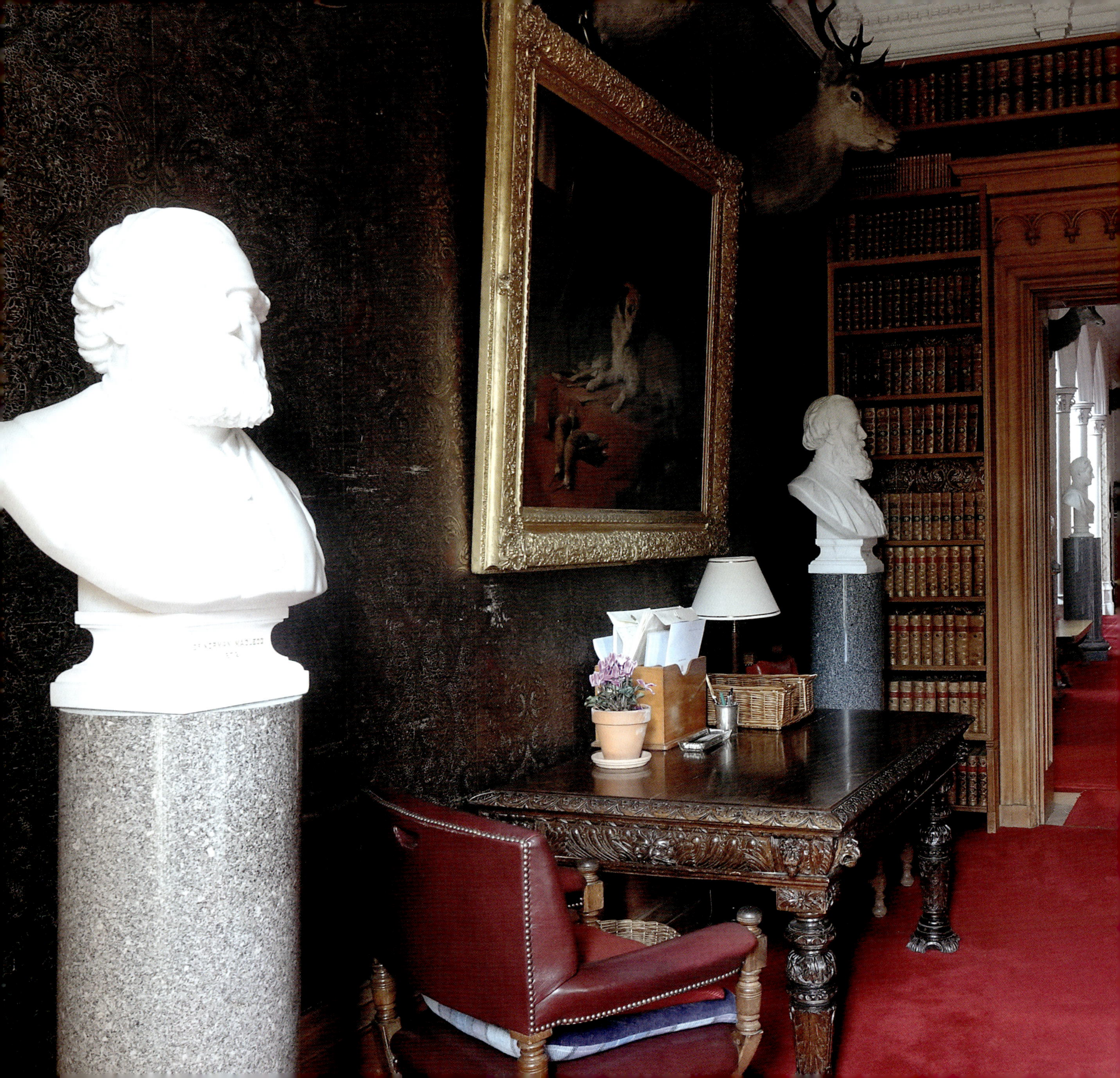

# The Vestibule

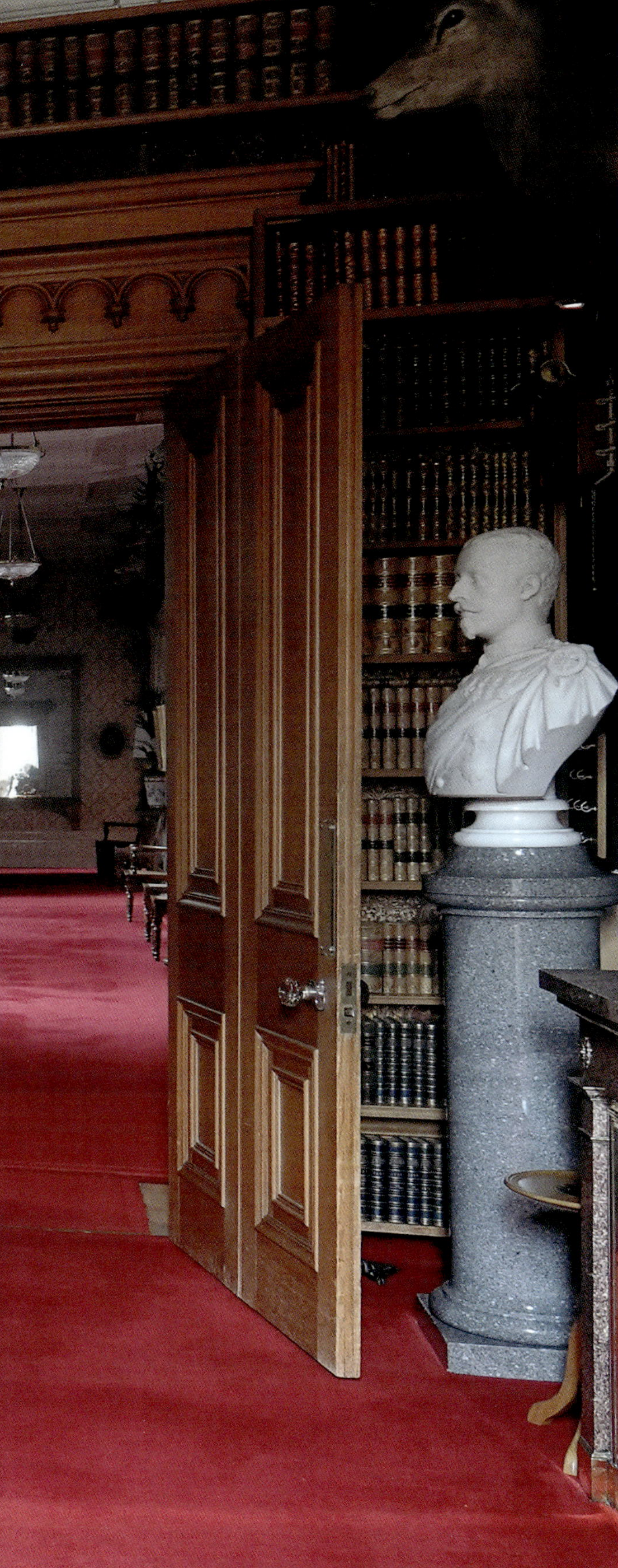

*left* View from the Vestibule looking down the Red Corridor. On the right is a bust of Prince Leopold, Duke of Albany, sculpted by Francis John Williamson in 1883. Queen Victoria commissioned this portrait of her youngest son to mark his marriage to Princess Helen of Waldeck and Pyrmont in 1882. He was a haemophiliac and sadly died in 1884.

The small ante-room connecting the main and family dining rooms is used during Court by the Page, the highest-ranking member of staff in the castle, who is present on call to Their Majesties 24 hours a day.

The Vestibule originally led out to the garden terrace, but the doorway was converted into a stained-glass window when Queen Victoria adapted the space as a private chapel (the coloured glass has since been removed). Lined with Ballochbuie pine, this 'service room' had a pulpit carved by the local woodworking class and engravings after Raphael. Its present appearance dates from around 1902, when Edward VII converted the room to its present role, introducing the embossed wallpaper and light fittings that survive (electricity had arrived in 1898).

More recently, The King has filled the previously empty shelves with books – examples include the philosopher Georg Hegel's 20-volume *Werke* (1840–54), which had a strong influence on Prince Albert's personal beliefs – and assembled the group of portrait busts of Royal princes and ministers of the Crathie Kirk. On the left, flanking Landseer's *Pen, Brush and Chisel: the Studio of Sir Francis Chantrey* (1835–36), are the Rev. John Tulloch (beside the door) and Queen Victoria's favourite minister, Dr Norman Macleod, author, Moderator of the Church of Scotland and grandfather of Lord Macleod, founder of the Iona Community. She commissioned the bust from John Hutchison in 1888.

# The Small Dining Room

This was originally the billiard room, its position between the drawing and dining rooms somewhat unusual given that billiard rooms were traditionally located in the male domain. A surviving fragment confirms that it was originally hung with the same blue and gold-stencilled wallpaper as the drawing room. The thistle motif recurs in the chintz curtains, which are copies of ones from Queen Victoria's sitting room.

Breakfast is served here, along with the old-fashioned teas that are still a feature of Highland shooting lodges – welcome sustenance to tide guests over until dinner following a bracing day on the hill. The tea service laid out over an Indian textile features photographs of Scotland taken by Queen Alexandra in 1891. She was introduced to porcelain decorated with transfers by her sister, the Tsarina, and this commission pioneered the technique in Britain.

The theme of His Majesty's picture hang is the landscape and sporting life that are central to Balmoral. The room celebrates the talents of Carl Haag, one of the artists summoned to come up in autumn and paint the local landscape, people and pursuits. The finest works to emerge from Haag's six-week visit in 1853 were his large companion watercolours *Morning in the Highlands* (p.10) and *Evening at Balmoral*. These have recently been moved to the room and displayed alongside four preparatory studies (p.14), which were brought up from Windsor in 2023 and placed in new maplewood frames.



*right* With its new Hunting Stewart carpet, thistle-sprigged chintz and landscape and sporting pictures, the room recaptures something of Holland & Sons' interiors. The satinwood cabinet belongs to the suite they made for the drawing room, on which the Highlander candelabra were displayed (p.13). The King's fondness for Wemyss Ware reflects that of his grandmother: the Queen Mother amassed one of the largest private collections, represented here by a pair of Tulip Vases by Robert Heron & Son of Kirkcaldy.

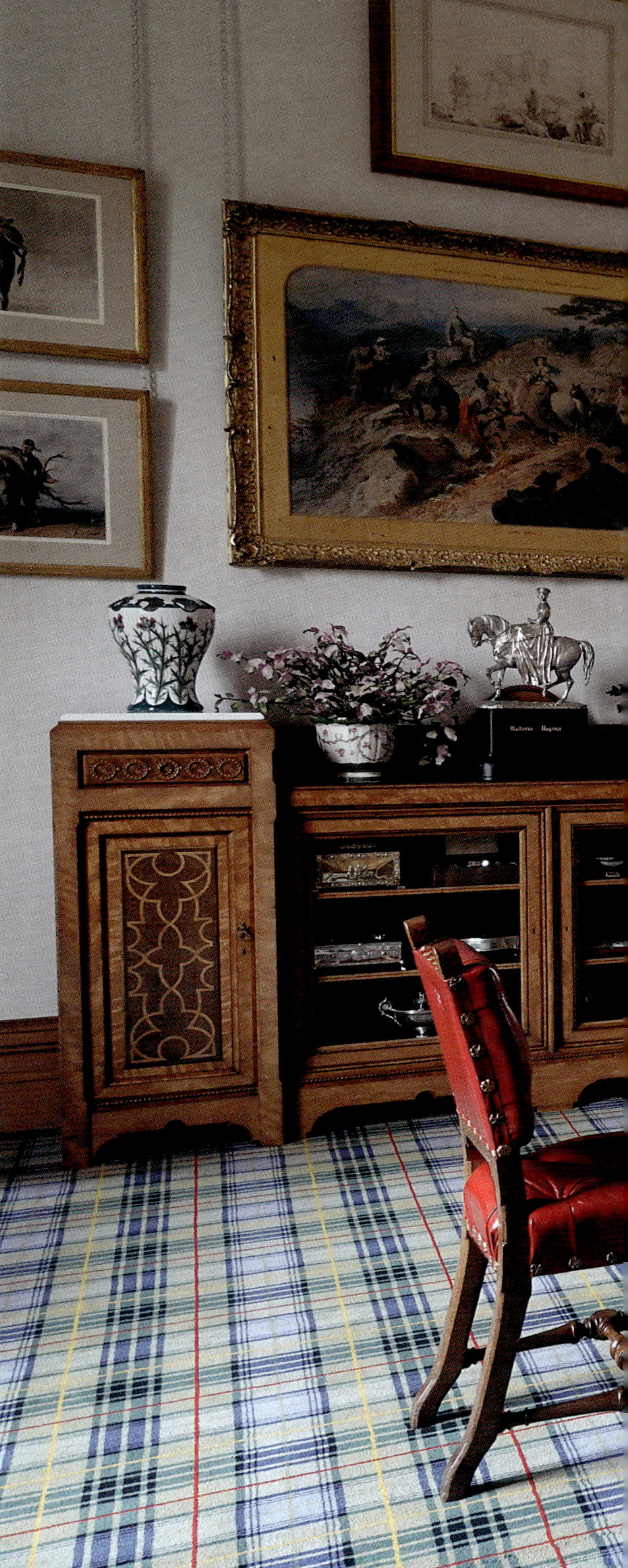

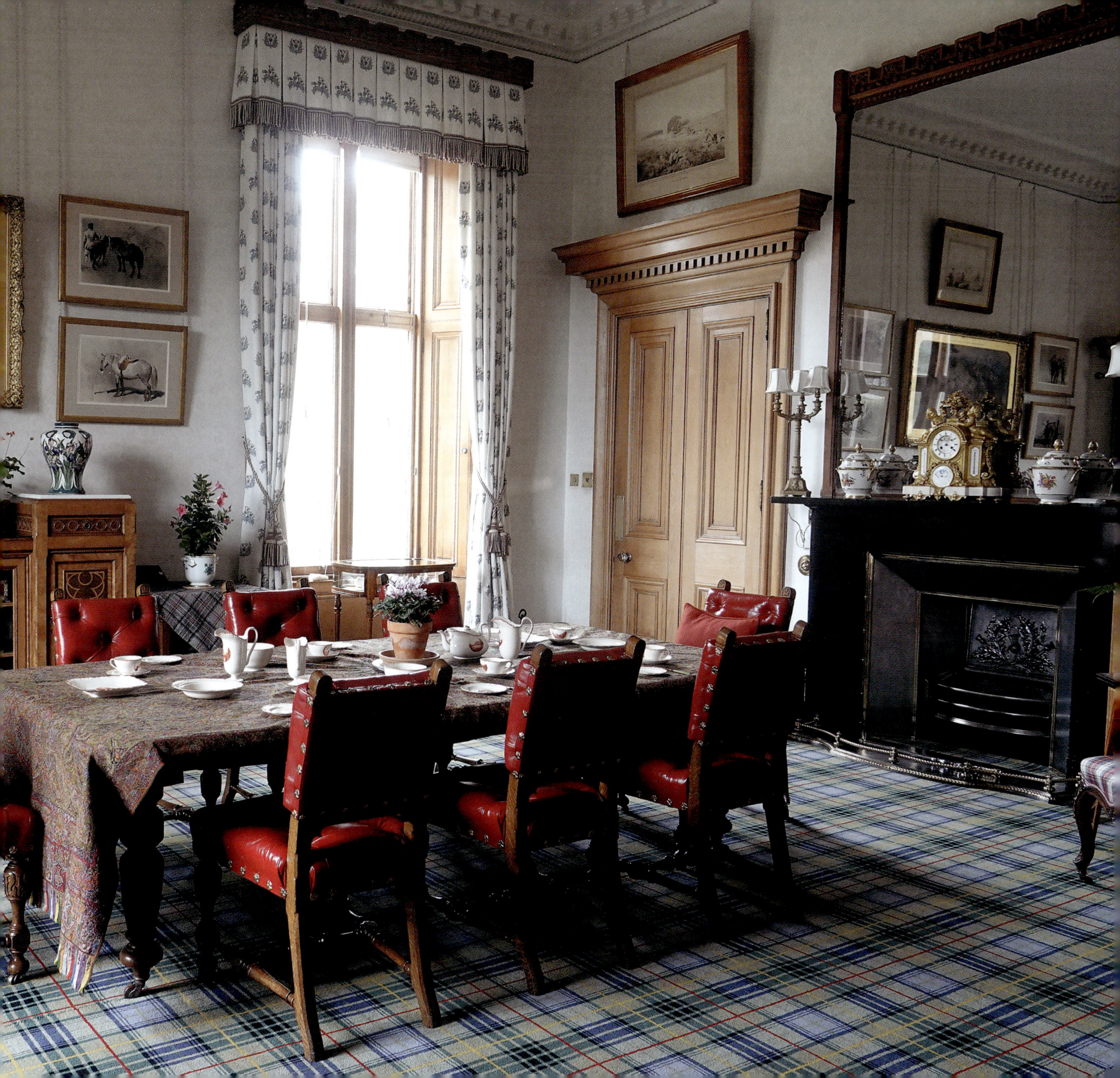

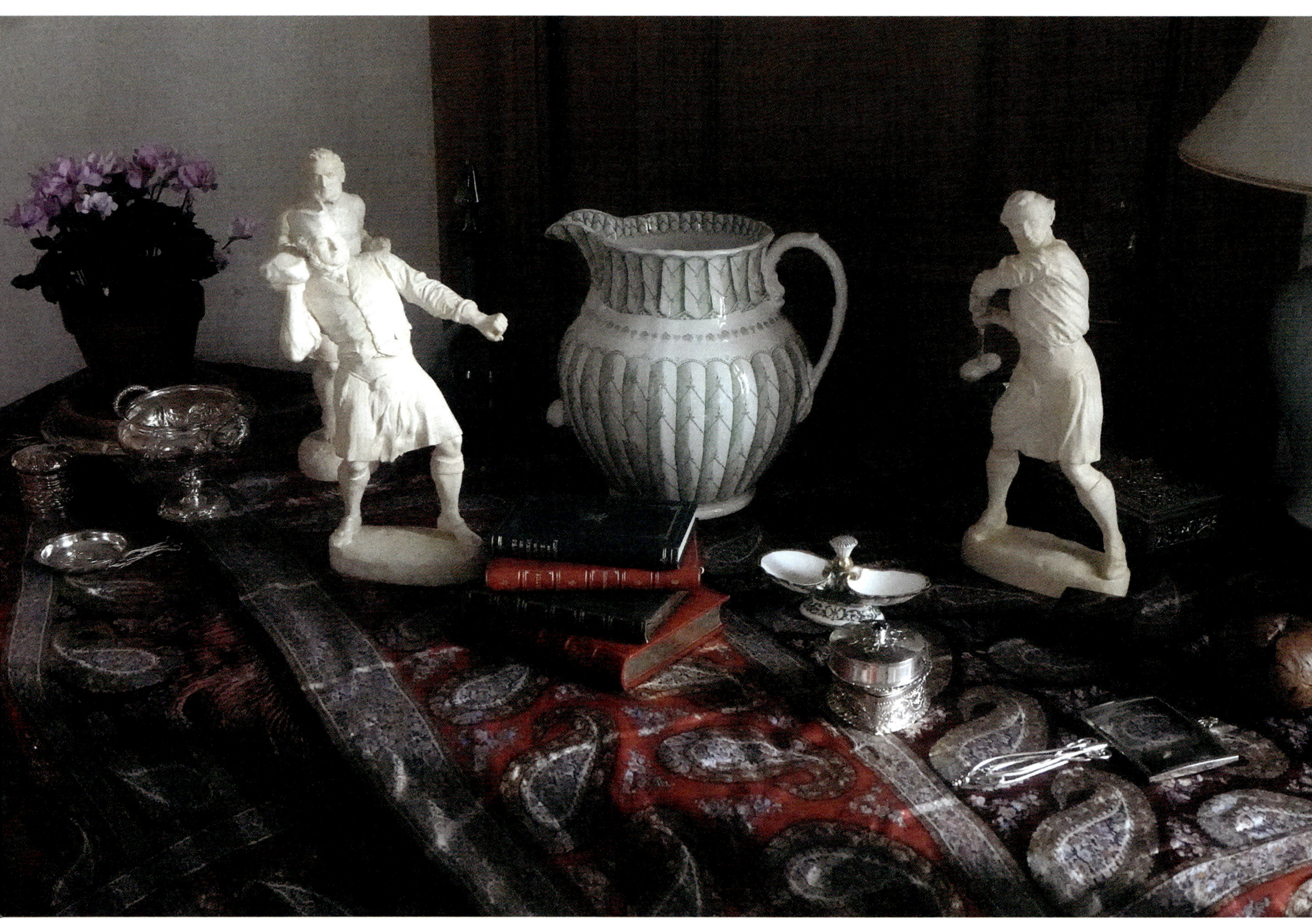

*above* Boehm's 1869 plaster-casts of figures engaged in athletic sports are among many idealised images of Highlanders at Balmoral and a reminder of the Highland games that reinvented their traditions. The objects are displayed on a Paisley throw, a typical detail introduced by The King, who loves to use textiles for added texture and colour.

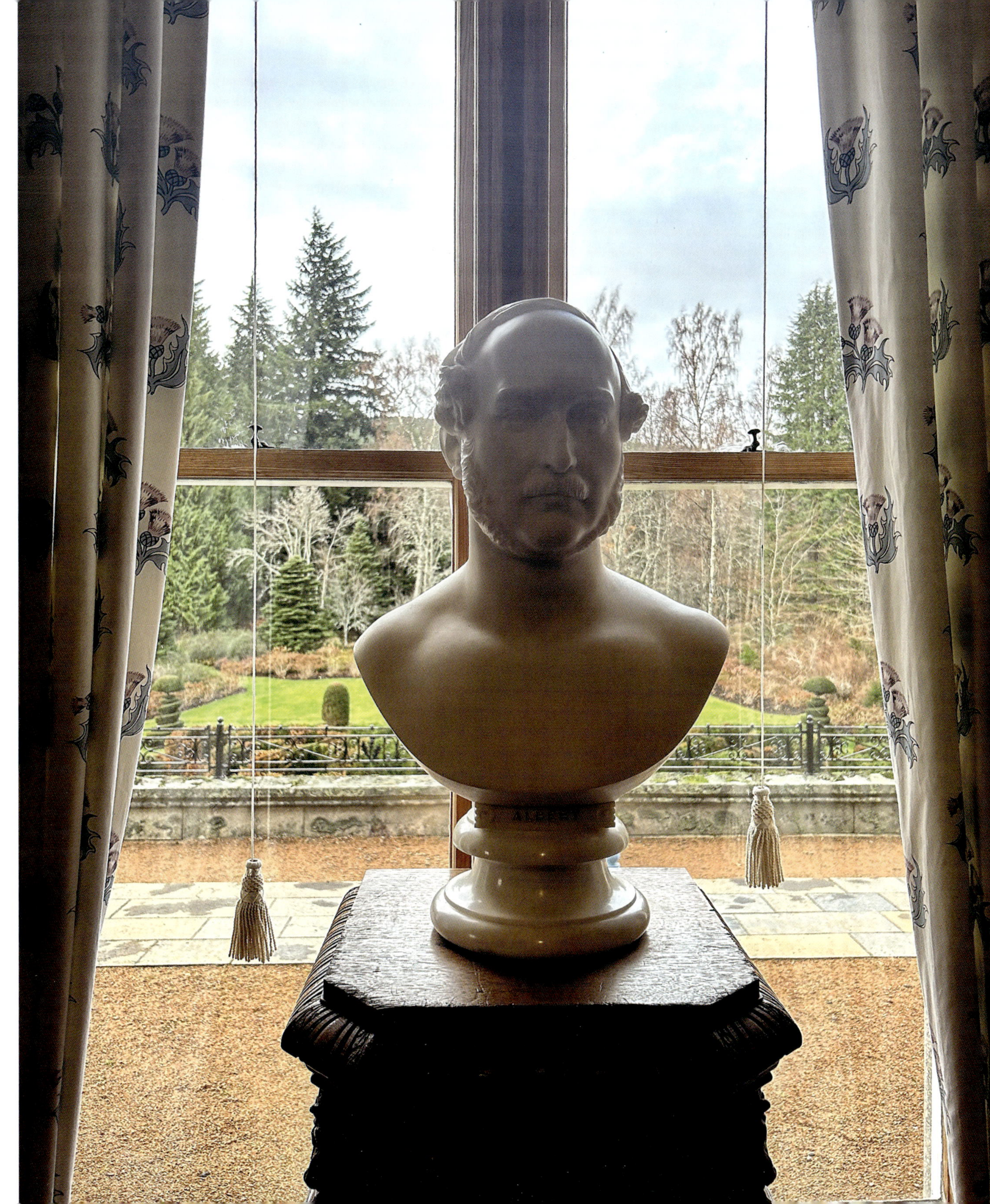

*right*  Queen Victoria commissioned William Theed to make this bust two weeks after Albert died in the Blue Room at Windsor Castle, where it was placed in 1862. His Majesty had it transferred here in 2023, and redisplayed the adjacent turret in homage to the Prince. The cabinet of mementos was brought down from the room above (formerly Albert's dressing room, which became a shrine) and displayed alongside objects and engravings of relevant interest.

# The Drawing Room

The drawing room revives the spirit of the original scheme, which was highly innovative for its mix of colour and pattern, comfortably upholstered sofas with light satinwood, birch and maple furniture, and elaborately designed pieces juxtaposed with animal and sporting prints.

His Majesty has introduced more decorative objects, such as the Parian Ware statuettes of Queen Victoria's children as the Seasons, and reorganised the furniture and pictures. Prince Albert's choice of engravings as more suitable than oil paintings for a sporting residence was adopted at many such Highland houses. The King has resurrected the fashion, adding an upper tier of sporting prints after Landseer. The artist is well represented among the paintings, too, with *Sunshine* and *Shadow*, contrasting the 'sunny' and 'dark' periods of Queen Victoria's life, flanking the overmantel mirror, portraits of Victoria and Albert's adored dogs, and the large-scale *Return from Stalking*, which Queen Elizabeth bought in 1945.

With textiles and cushions refreshed, more ceramics, and plentiful plants and flowers when Their Majesties are in residence, the room has a bright, contemporary look that feels remarkably compatible with the original aesthetic.

*right* Modern Hunting Stewart (carpets) and Dress Stewart tartans have replaced the bland green 1980s decor. Among the decorative objects that have recently been introduced are a goldfish jardinière by Minton and Wemyss Ware vases flanking the Regency ormulu-mounted Boulle bracket clock on the mantelpiece.



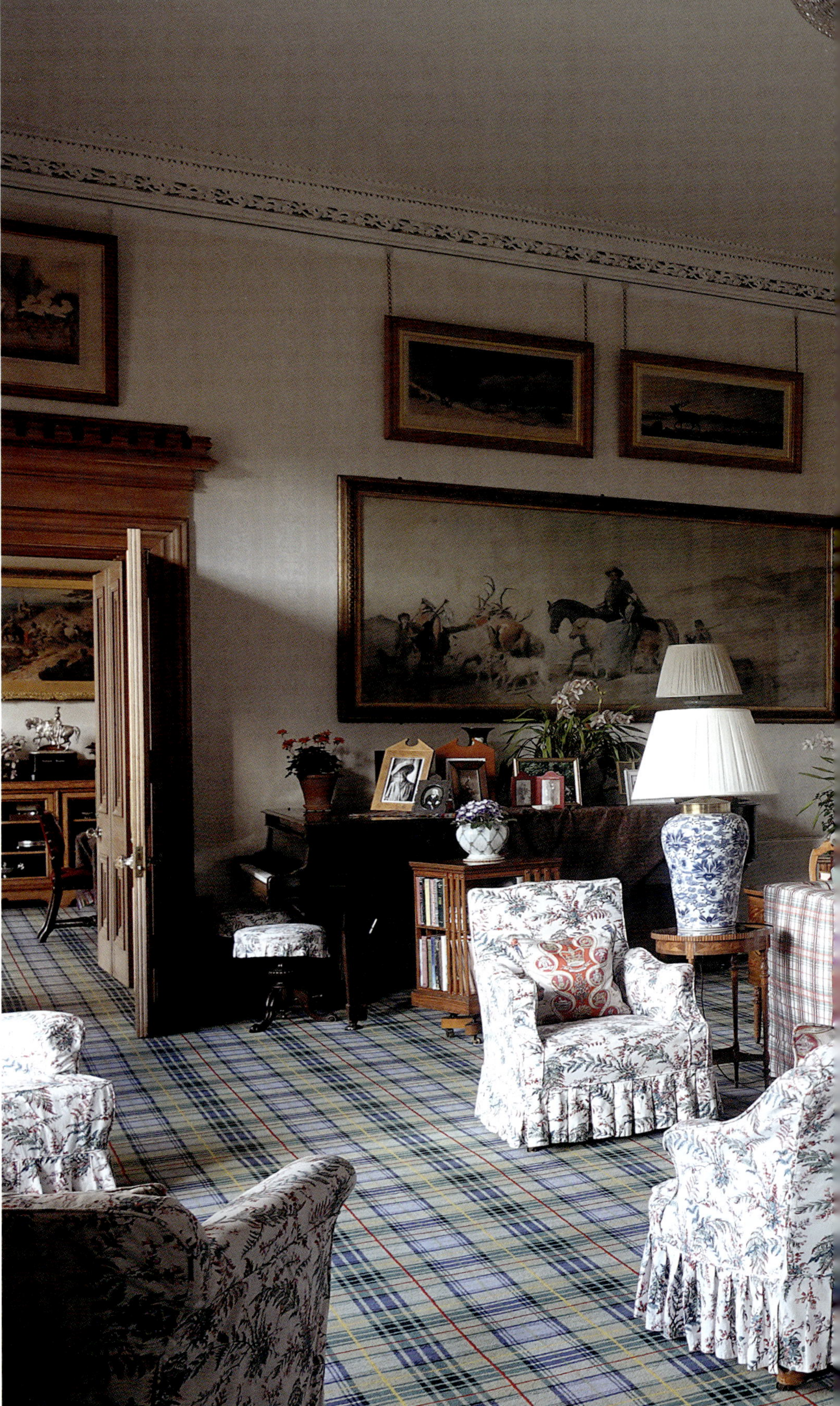

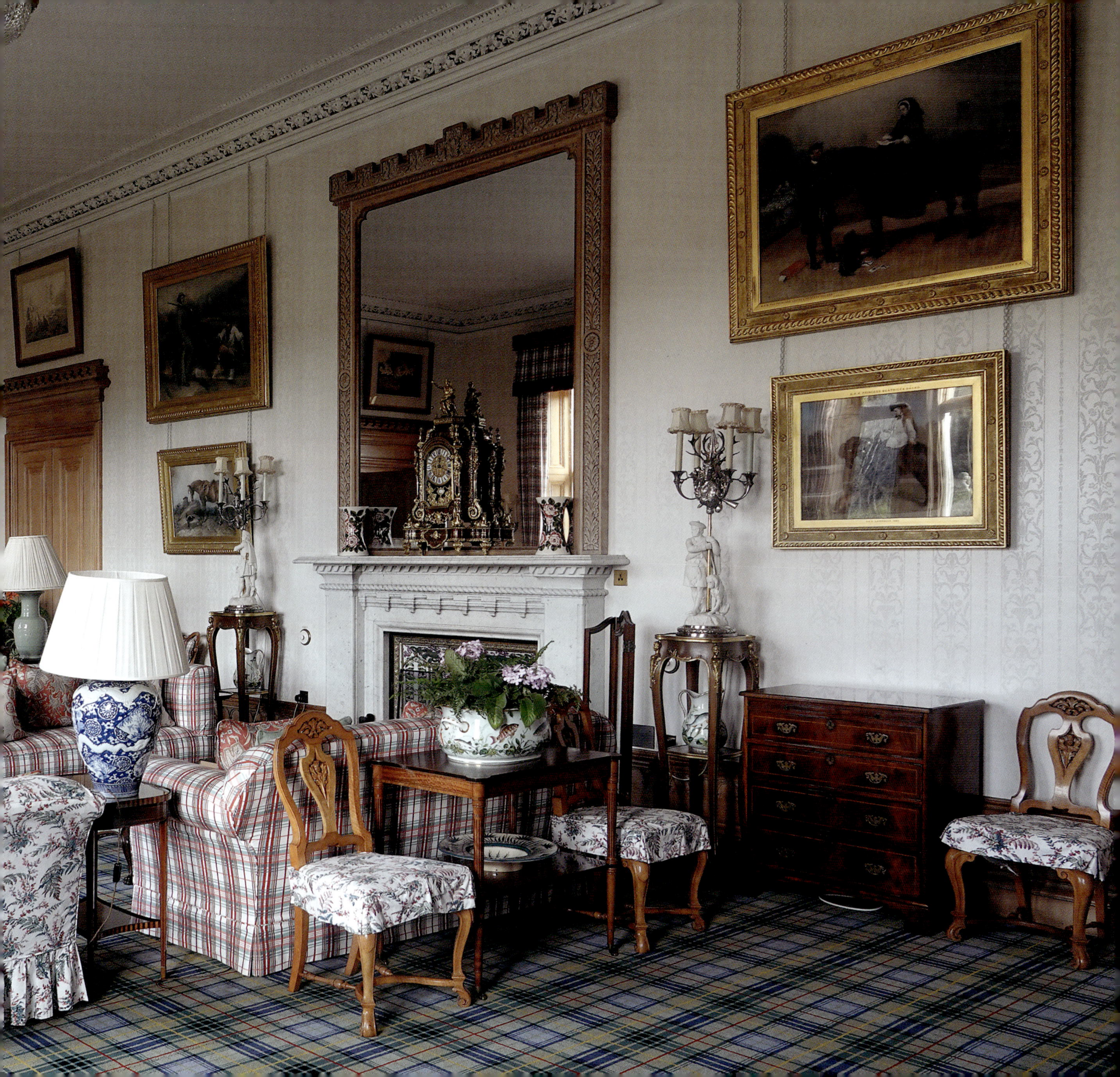

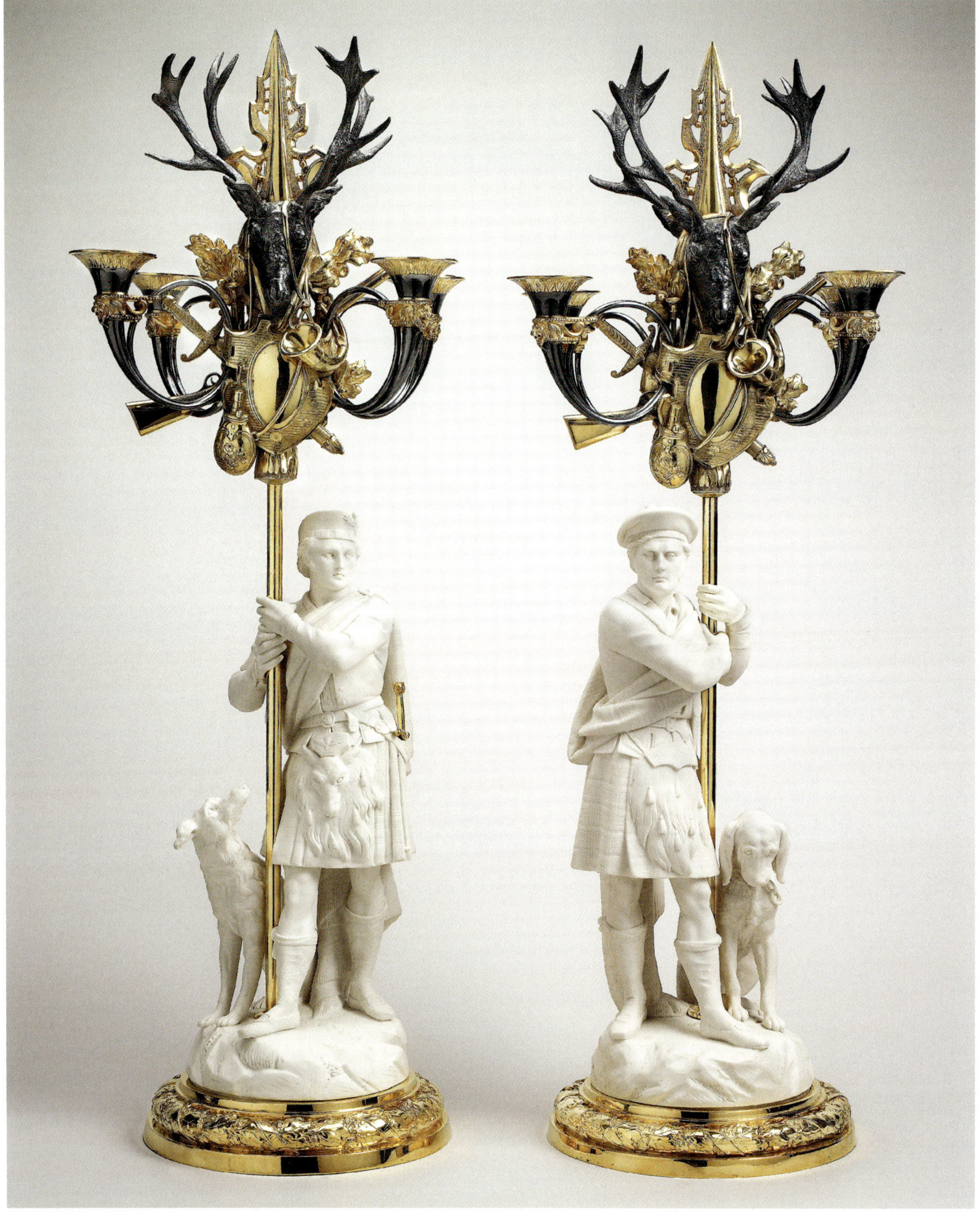

*left*  Queen Victoria commissioned a set of 12 candelabra for the drawing room and gave them to Prince Albert for his birthday. Made in 1854 by the leading manufacturers Minton of Stoke-on-Trent and Winfield of Birmingham, they take the form of a Highlander with deerhound or bloodhound, modelled in Parian to Landseer's design, holding elaborate metalwork stalking trophies. They stood on Holland & Sons' satinwood cabinets, as depicted in James Roberts's 1857 watercolour (p.13).

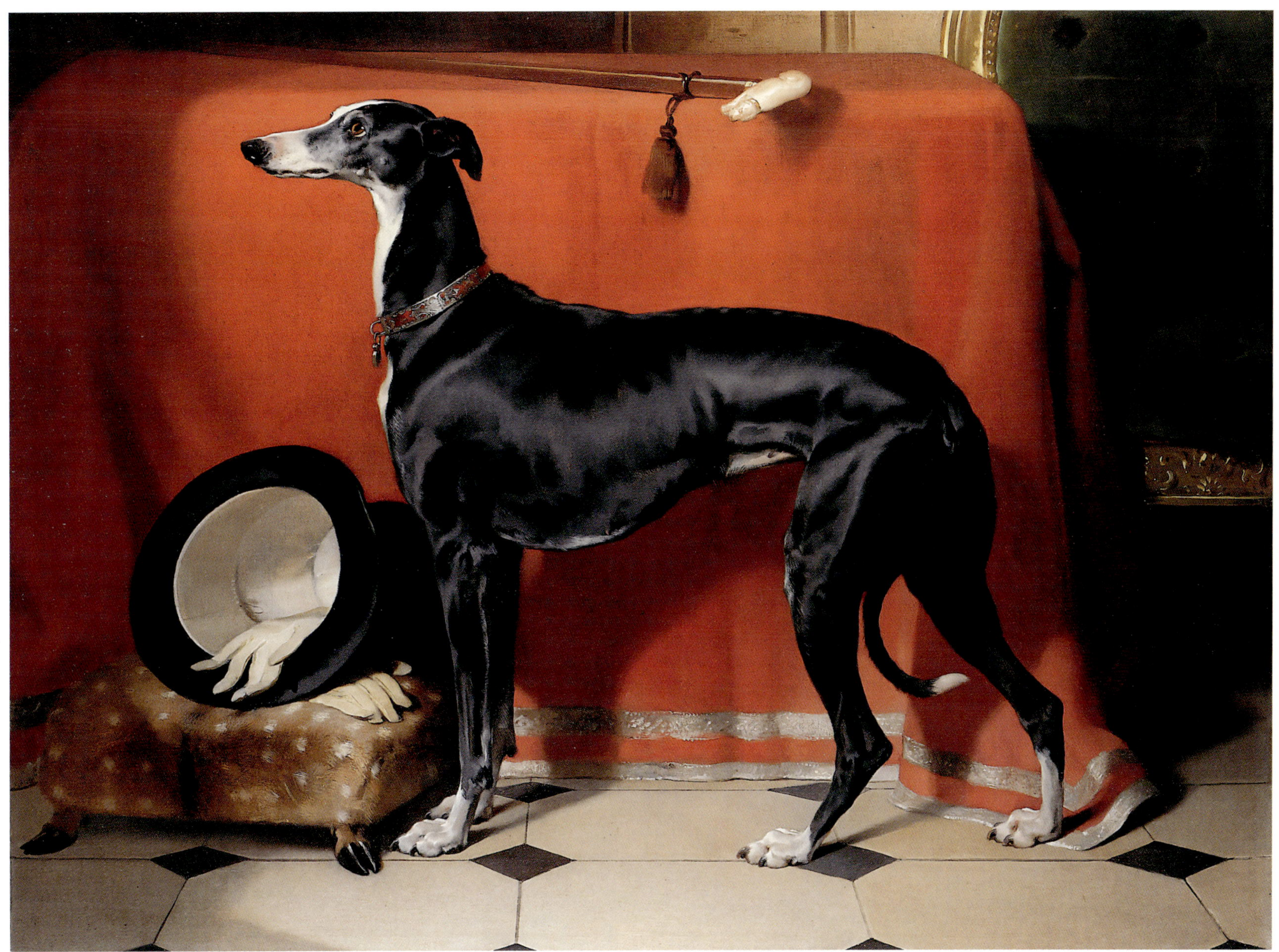

*abovw* Landseer's supremely elegant portrait shows Albert's beloved greyhound Eos, who accompanied her master when he first arrived in England in 1840 and was 'a constant and faithful companion for 10½ years ... connected with the happiest years of his life', recorded Victoria, who gave the painting to Albert for Christmas 1841. His Majesty has recently had the walking cane brought up from Windsor and displayed underneath the painting.

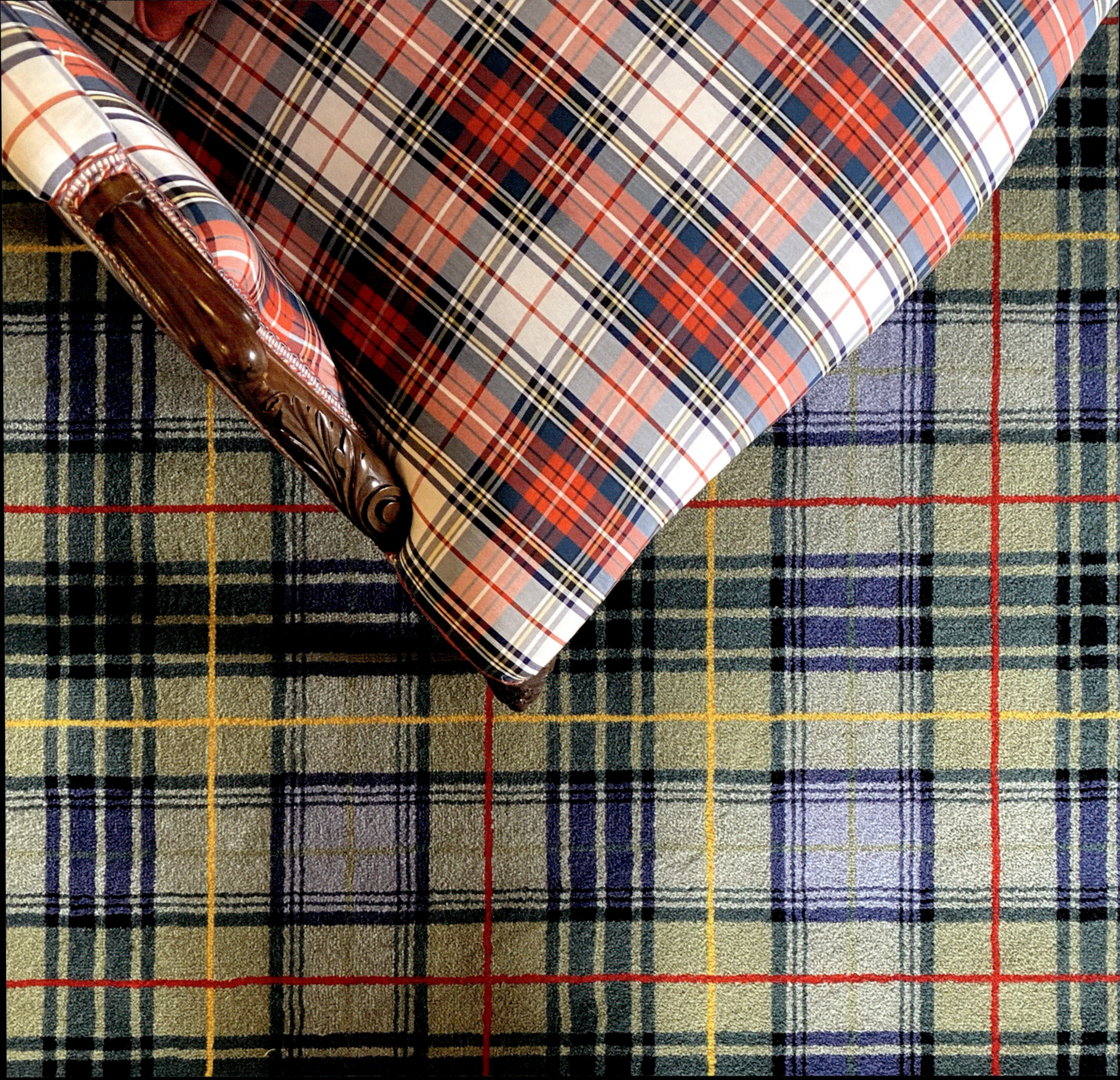

# Balmoral: the Tartan Tastemaker

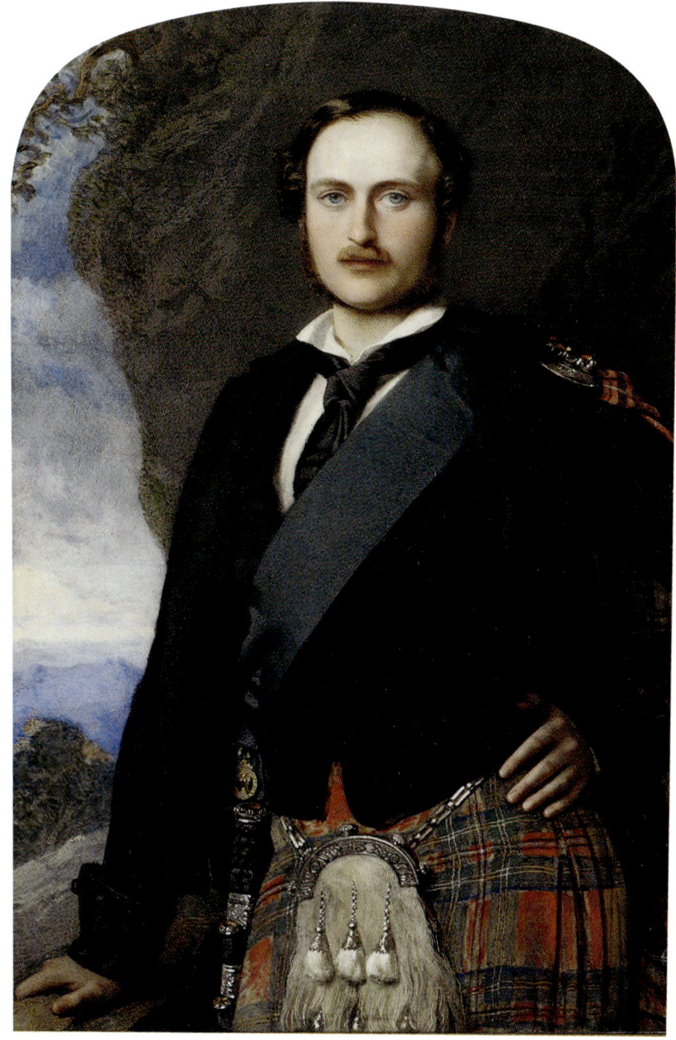

*left* After a period of derision in the 20th century, tartan decoration is fashionable again and has recently been reintroduced to Balmoral in brighter palettes. The carpets are woven in Hunting Stewart, the chair upholstered in Victoria, or Dress, Stewart.

*right* Prince Albert commissioned this watercolour on ivory as a birthday present for the Queen. Painted in 1852 by the leading miniaturist Robert Thorburn, it shows him in a kilt of Royal Stewart and the ribbon of the Order of the Thistle. Albert had first donned a kilt at Ardverikie in 1847, which he wore 'with a dark green doublet & plaid, pouch & dirk & his Garter over his stocking, looking so handsome, as my dear Treasure ever does', as his wife recorded. The following year at Balmoral, he was late for dinner owing to his 'struggles to dress in a kilt'.

Tartan was the keynote of Balmoral, used decoratively and sartorially for symbolic and aesthetic effect. Curtains, carpets and upholstery pulsed with the varying colourways of Royal, Hunting and Dress Stewart – even the servants' linoleum was plaided. For the Queen, it was a tangible connection to her Stewart roots, but it also put Balmoral at the forefront of taste, reflecting the ideas of the Edinburgh design reformers, who favoured geometric pattern as a clean, bright, modern alternative to three-dimensional Georgian motifs.

Following a period of complex and conflicting symbolism during the rebellious 18th century, tartan dress had undergone a revival among the upper classes and was particularly fashionable for dresses, shawls and children's outfits. Queen Victoria's enthusiasm was pivotal to the widening of its popularity, and to its commodification for everything from clothing and upholstery to Mauchline Ware souvenirs. Pushing aside the irony of its proscription by her ancestor after 1745, she and her ladies wore tartan shawls and scarves at Balmoral, the Princes kilts in Balmoral or Hunting Stewart, with Royal Stewart for the evenings. The Queen favoured Dress Stewart, a variation of Royal Stewart with the broad red band changed to white. First produced by Wilsons of Bannockburn in 1838, it became hugely popular as the 'Victoria' tartan. The Balmoral, designed by Prince Albert for the Royal Household, was a version of Royal Stewart, woven in shades of black, red and lavender on a marled grey ground to represent the rugged Grampian terrain.

Inspired by Lord Breadalbane's Highlanders and the keepers at Mar, the Queen instituted Highland garb for her gillies and stalkers. They wore kilts of Balmoral tartan, with jackets and bonnets of Balmoral tweed – as seen in Haag's watercolours (p.14). Balmoral had one of the first estate tweeds, its mid-grey (navy and white blended) ground, sprinkled with red, providing camouflage against the granite landscape. Designed by Albert, it was first woven by Johnstons of Elgin in 1853.

# The Library

Situated between the entrance hall and the drawing room on the castle's west front, this room did not always look so comfortable. James Roberts's 1857 view shows it with the usual tartan and thistle-sprigged livery, but sparsely furnished, with just a small table laid for a meal and some leather Chesterfields round the sides. Despite the distance from the kitchens, Victoria and Albert often had breakfast and lunch here and Victoria dined and received visitors here in later years.

Today, the room is furnished in a relaxed, eclectic style that mixes decorative objects and Boehm's busts of Royal and literary figures with chintz upholstery, tartan curtains and a richly coloured 'Turkey' carpet. Their Majesties' love of chintz echoes that of Queen Victoria, who adopted this aspect of the Old Balmoral interiors. With the introduction of more reading lamps and cushions, as well as plants, the library now feels like a comfortable study-sitting room.

The bookcases reflect Holland & Sons' pale-wood aesthetic. (The woodwork at Balmoral was sacrificed to an all-pervading 'marmalade-coloured paint' in the 1880s, but Queen Mary stripped it as soon as she could.) Filling the shelves is an outstanding collection that reflects, in particular, the Royal Family's interest in Scotland. Established by Victoria and Albert, who acquired around 6,000 of the 10,000 books and manuscripts at Balmoral, it includes antiquarian works, Stewart histories, poetry and novels, sporting literature and books on customs, natural history and conservation.



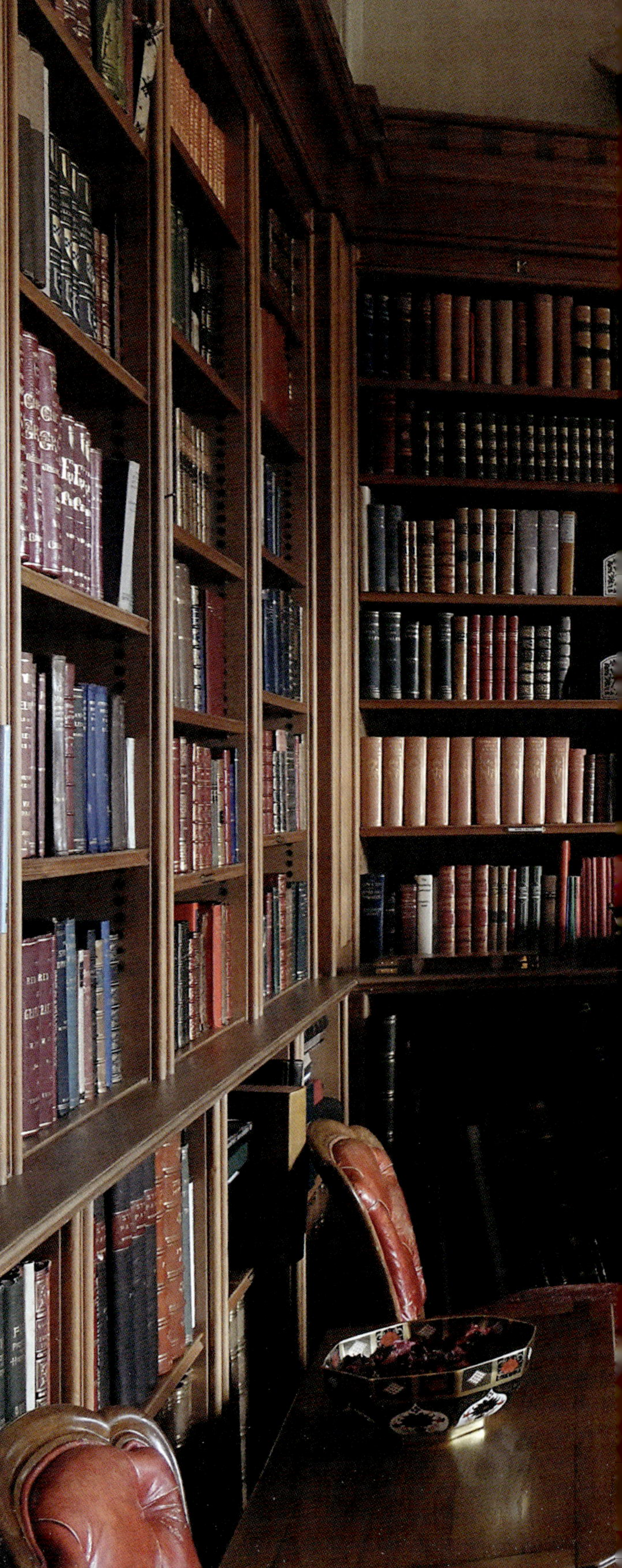

*right* The library, lined with a book collection created by Victoria and Albert, has recently been enhanced with newly introduced objects and furnishings to make it a comfortable room in which to relax, study and read.

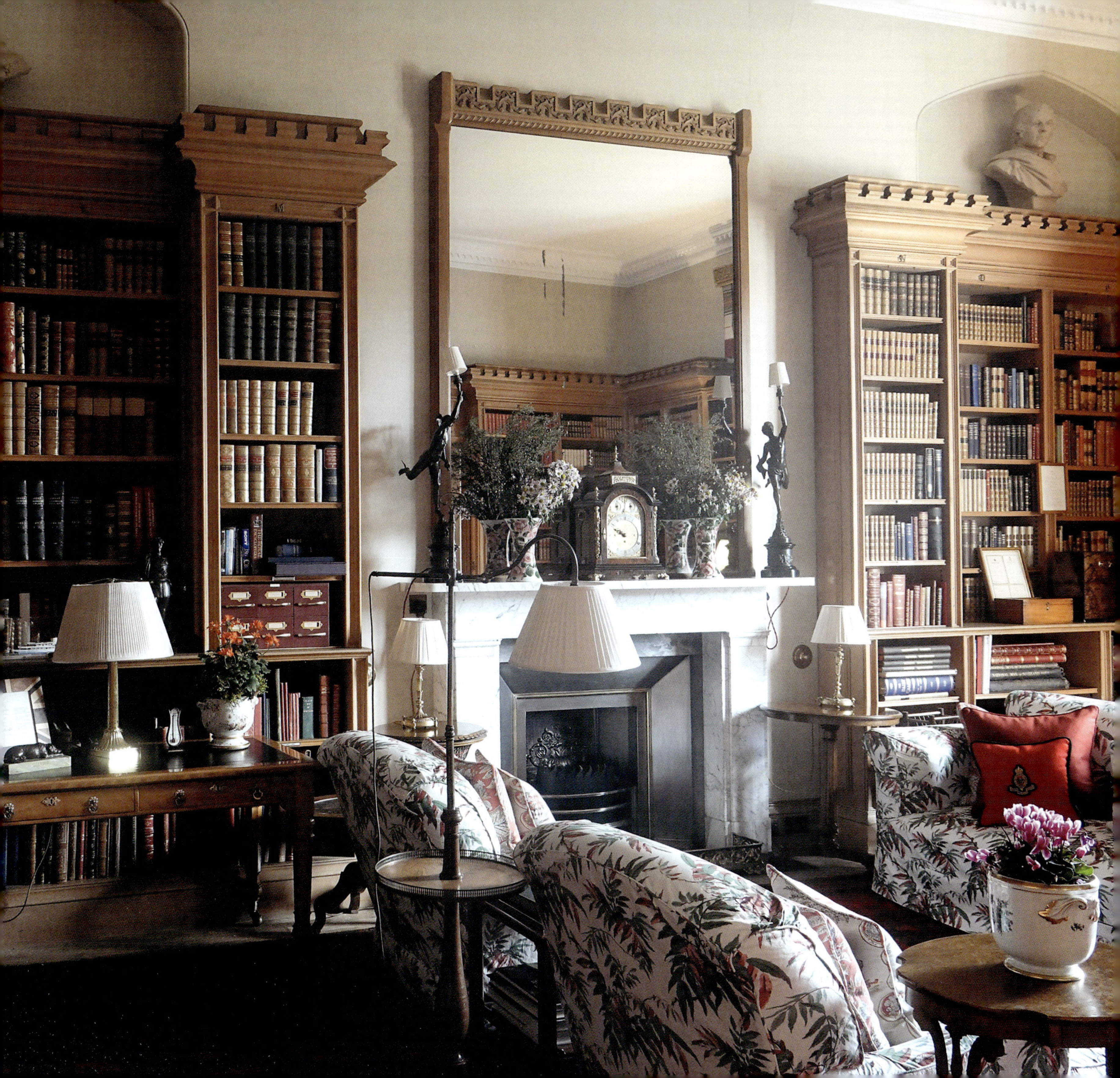

Unsurprisingly, given that the first novel Queen Victoria read was *The Bride of Lammermoor*, Scott's work features in multiple editions, including a luxury 1866 production of *Marmion*, illustrated with Thomas Annan's photographs and bound in wood from Flodden Field. One guest reported that there were 32 copies of *The Lady of the Lake* and 12 of *Rob Roy* dispersed throughout the castle.

Ranging from the 16th to the present century, the collection includes *Scottish Poems* (1792), with pieces by James I of Scotland, George IV's copy of *The Works of Robert Burns* (1809) and books in Gaelic and the local Doric vernacular. There are also significant publications on local botany, and *The Highlanders of Scotland*, filled with Kenneth Macleay's portraits commissioned by Queen Victoria.

The focus is not solely Scottish. Many international authors and playwrights are represented, as are social issues such as the treatment of Indian and Chinese immigrants in England, the lives of Parsis in India and the experiences of Jews in Russia. In 1859, Victoria and Albert established a lending library for estate staff, personally selecting edifying books for their moral and scientific education.

George V and Queen Mary countered Edward VII's dismissal of the library as 'the mausoleum of the great unread' by augmenting the collection with the help of Rev. John Stirton – the role of Balmoral librarian was traditionally held by the minister. The late Queen's additions included contemporary novels, histories and books on natural history, landscape and conservation.



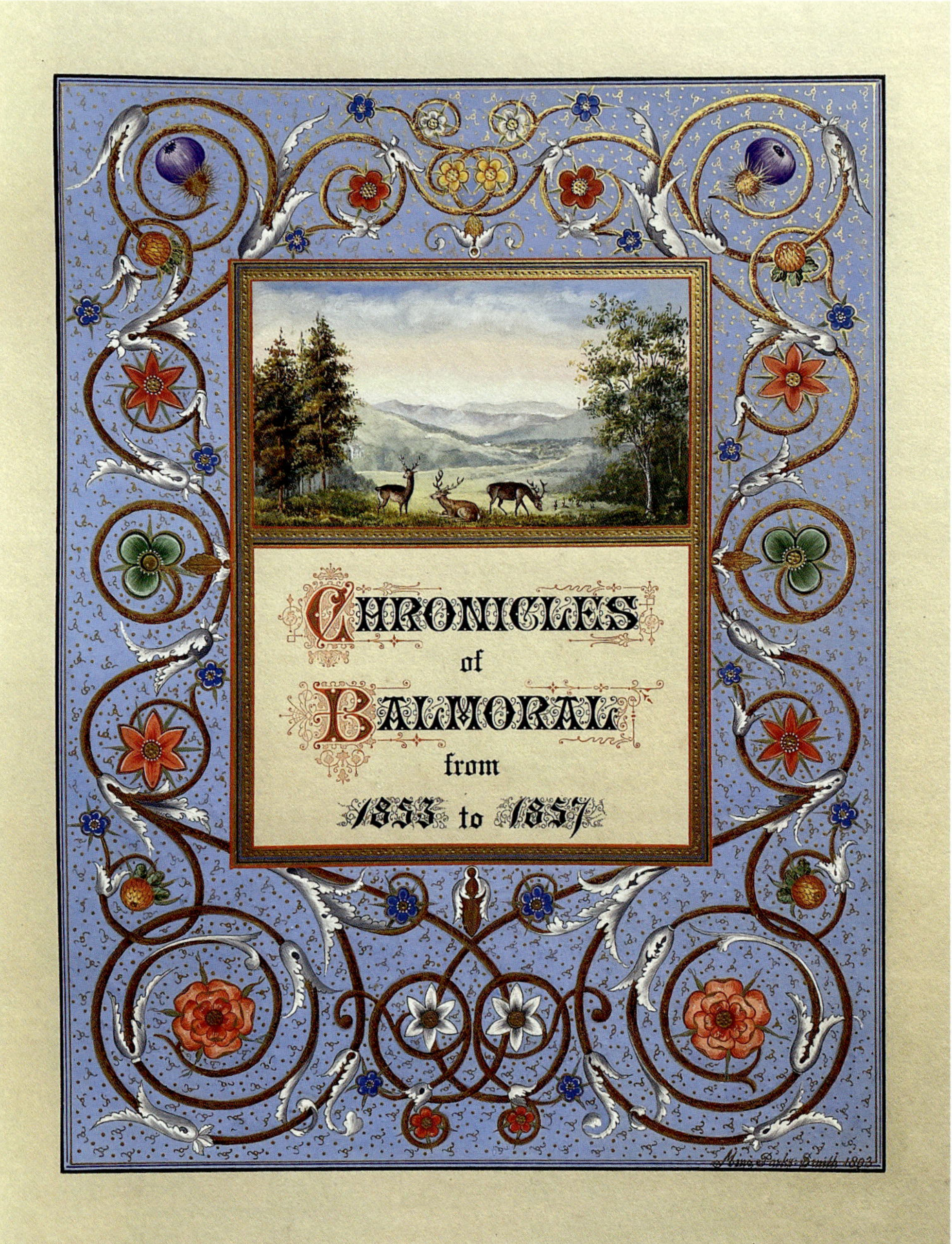

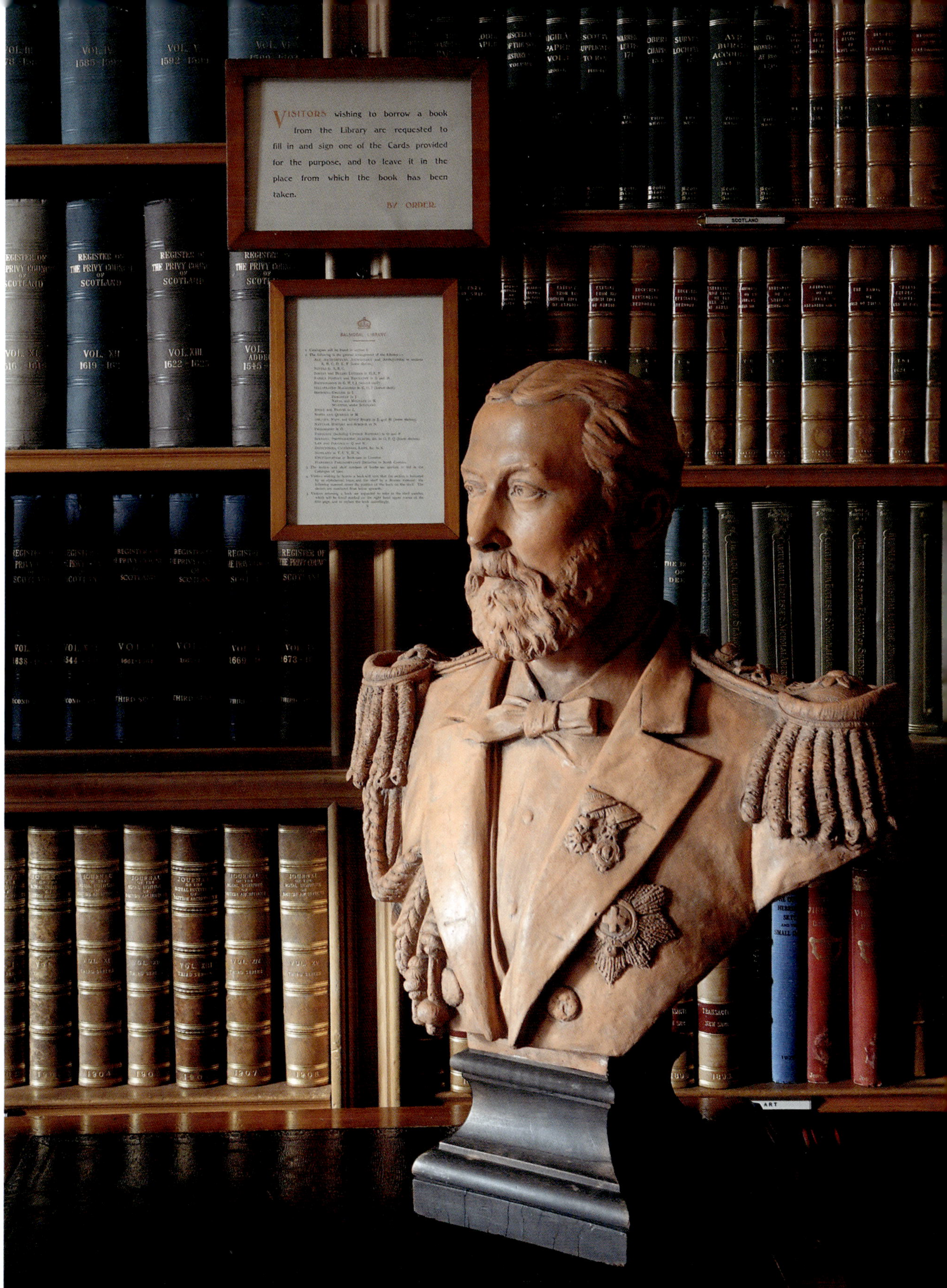

*left*  One of four volumes by Mina Parks-Smith, an artist/calligrapher who was tutor to Princess Beatrice. They contain illuminated descriptions of activities and events that took place during Royal holidays here and include beautiful illustrations of flowers and wildlife.

*right*  His Majesty has introduced Boehm's terracotta bust of Prince Alfred, Queen Victoria's fourth child, who died six months before her. The Prince became Duke of Edinburgh and, in 1893, succeeded his uncle Ernst II as Duke of Saxe-Coburg and Gotha. Pinned to the bookcase above is an order requesting visitors who borrow a book to fill in and sign a card and leave it on the shelf in place of the book.

# The Ballroom

'There used to be a considerable amount of dancing; one of the gillies played the pipes, and we used to dance to their music, servants and all,' recalled Georgiana Swinton, whose family rented Balmoral in the early 1840s. Queen Victoria was similarly enchanted by the balls she attended at neighbouring Corriemulzie, where Highlanders and gentry performed reels and sword dances by torchlight. Such events were typically held in simple dancehalls, such as the one installed at Balmoral in 1851 – a pre-fabricated structure designed for emigrants' housing that Albert had seen at the Great Exhibition. One of the world's earliest surviving corrugated-iron buildings, it is now a workshop on the estate.

It was replaced by a rugged, castellated, Tudor-Gothic range rising from lower ground at right angles to the castle, from where it screens the kitchens from the north terraces. The interior, decorated by the impresario Thomas Grieve, was a medieval fantasy in a similar vein to Taymouth Castle, which had crystallised Scottishness for Queen Victoria when she stayed there in 1842. An engraving of the Grand Ball in Taymouth's Banner Hall, where she danced with the velvet-plaided Marquess, suggests Grieve's inspiration for the Balmoral ballroom's theatrical displays of weaponry and sporting trophies, heraldic carving and painted ceiling, tartan draperies and Puginian chandeliers (p.11).

The gillies' ball remains an annual tradition, albeit one less rowdy than the whisky-fuelled events instituted by Queen Victoria.

*right* Built in 1856, the ballroom was originally accessed from the north terrace (the linking passage was added later) and is entered at the upper level, from where stairs lead down from a balustraded platform. It was fitted out by Thomas Grieve in time for the 1858 gillies' ball, with a mirrored Gothic alcove for the Royal party carved with heraldry and richly traceried niches in satin birchwood. Edward VII had the compartmented ceiling repainted with Royal ciphers and national plants.

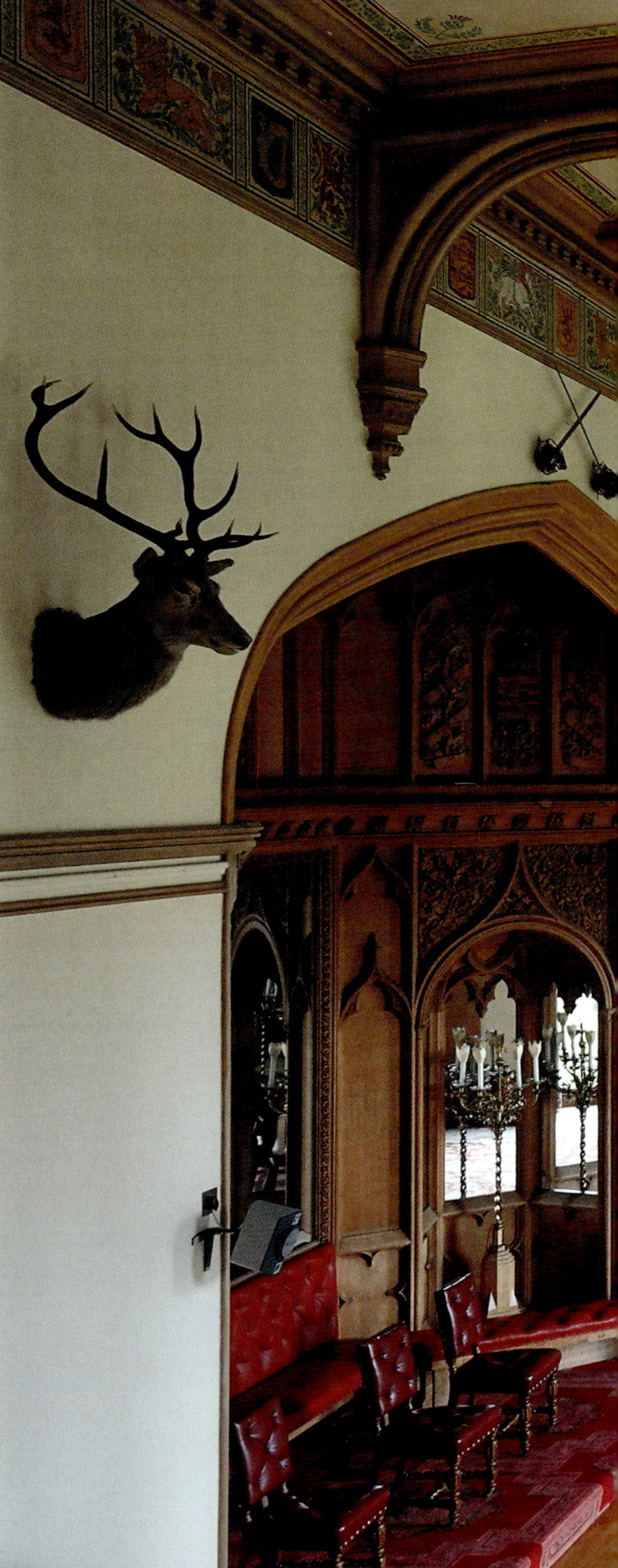

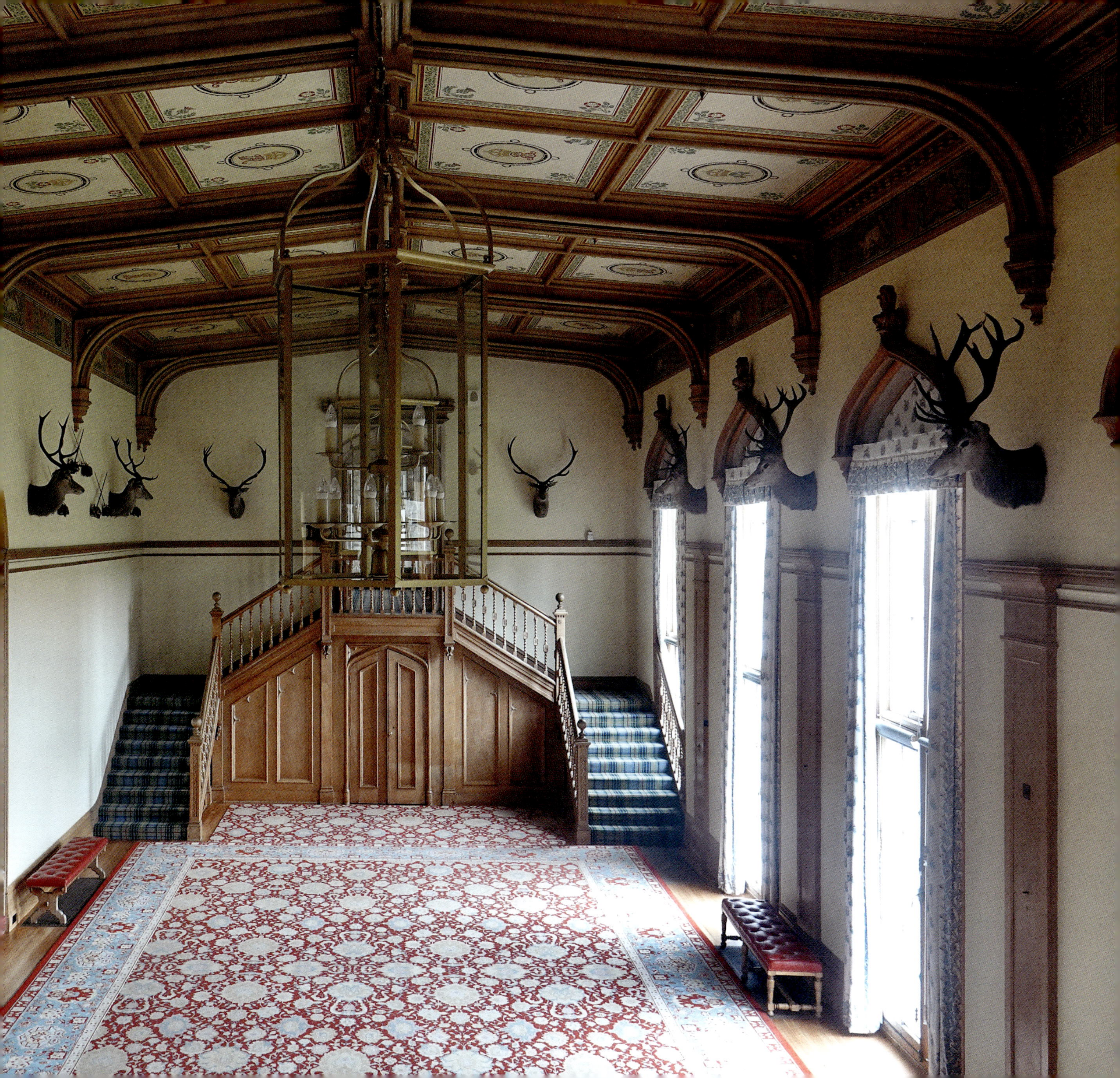

# Landseer at Balmoral

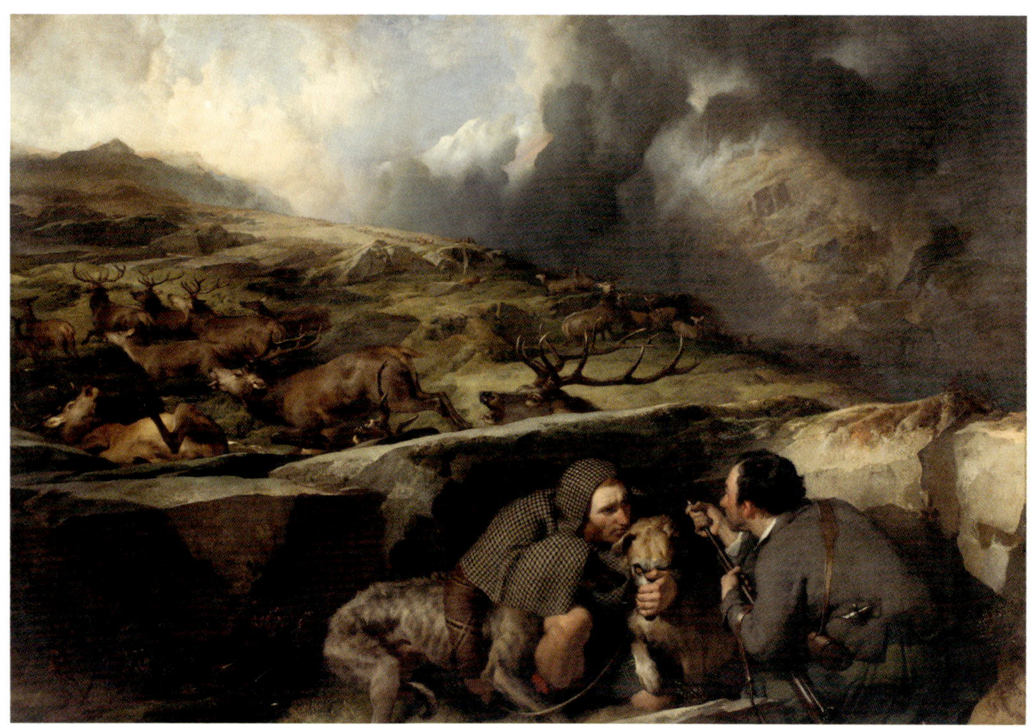

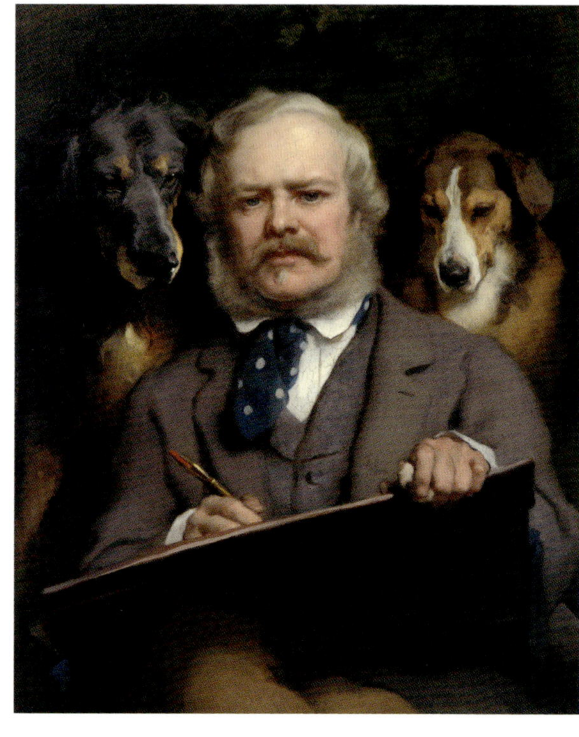

Sir Edwin Landseer was the pre-eminent animal painter of his day and Victoria and Albert's favourite artist. Together, they helped to immortalise the Highlands as a Sublime wilderness in which man and Nature are united and the traditions of a nobler past preserved. It was a Highlands romanticised by their hero Sir Walter Scott, populated by hunting chieftains, loyal Highlanders and magnificent beasts.

Landseer first met the Queen in 1837, and would go on to paint many portraits of her family and pets. He had first visited the Highlands in 1824, and became a convivial guest at his patrons' shooting lodges, including Balmoral in Sir Robert Gordon's day and Ardverikie, where he 'learned all his deer-lore' and muralled the dining-room walls. In 1847, he visited Victoria and Albert at Ardverikie and accepted his first Royal commission on a Highland theme: *Queen Victoria Sketching at Loch Laggan* (p.12).

Scotland would provide the setting for many of Landseer's most significant works. The dazzling virtuosity with which he painted stags – regal, dead or dying – in exhilarating mountain landscapes elevated sporting art into a new realm. Albert's admiration is reflected at Balmoral in his choice of prints, the medium through which Landseer's art was widely popularised. His genre

*above left* Looming over the staircase, *The Deer-Drive* (1847) depicts the 'good old feudal style' of *battue* that Lord Breadalbane planned for Albert in Glenorchy forest, the rifles hiding in the foreground.

*above* Landseer presented his self-portrait to Edward VII (then Prince of Wales) in 1867. Titled *The Connoisseurs*, it shows his collie dog and a retriever appearing to judge his work.

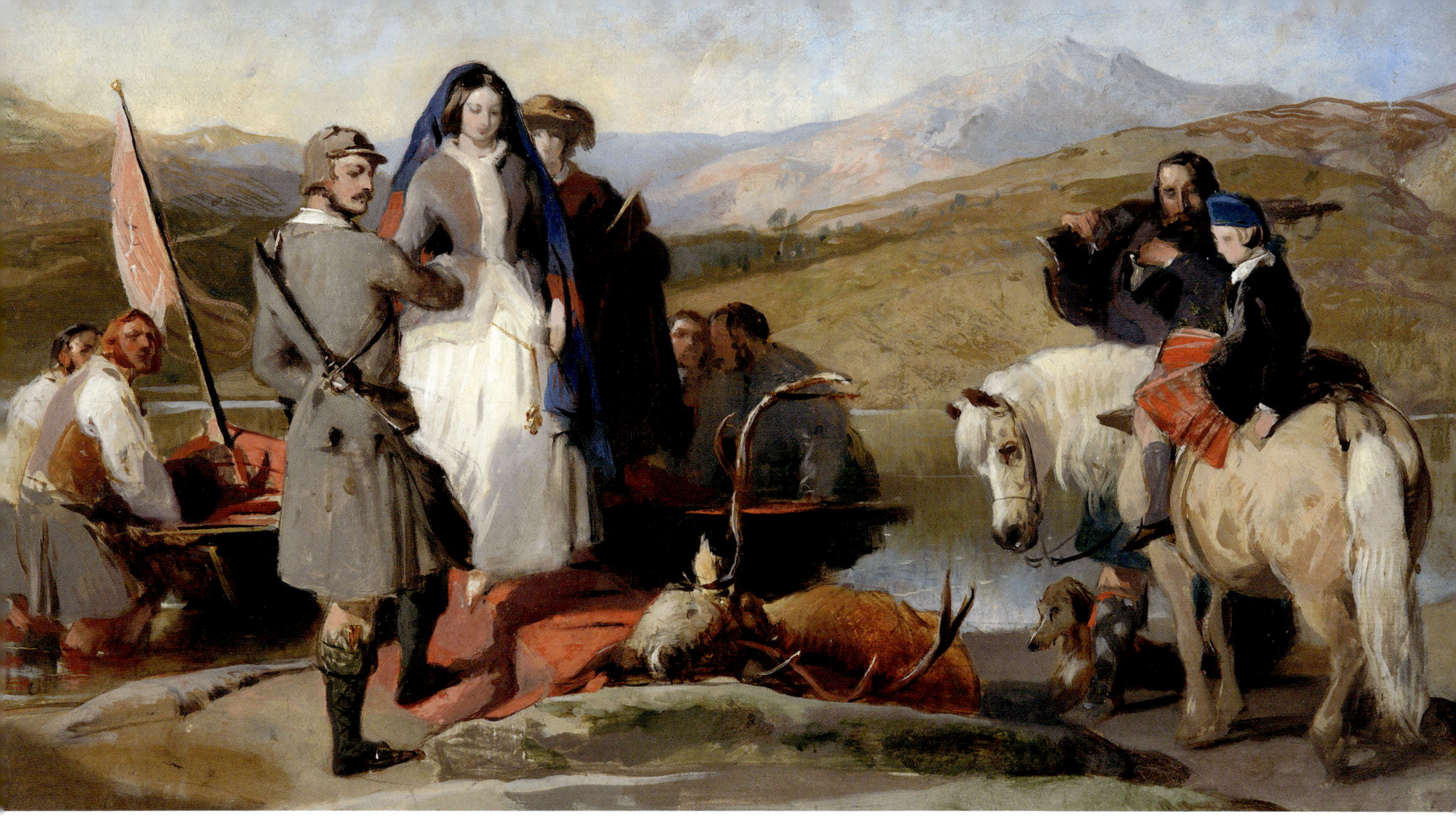



scenes helped to shape the Victorian image of the strong, loyal Highlander and rosy-cheeked lassie, living in picturesque poverty but not destitute. Some criticised him for turning a blind eye to the realities of the rural crisis and for glamorising and sentimentalising the Highlands.

The Queen invited Landseer to Balmoral in September 1850, and commissioned him to do a painting inspired by *The Lady of the Lake* and her experience of being rowed by kilted oarsmen up Loch Muick. She watched him make skilful studies of her gillies and was confident he would capture 'the beauty, poetry, and wildness of the scene'. But *Royal Sports on Hill and Loch* was to prove a disaster, delayed and reworked over 15 years and causing Landseer a near breakdown. None of his paintings of the Royal Family in Scotland attained his usual brio, but the Queen was loyal to him and invited him back, lastly in 1867, when he completed some drawings, but felt wretched and couldn't sleep. He died, mentally disturbed, in 1873.

# The Gardens at Balmoral

Surrounding the castle and extending along the Dee lie 120 acres of policies with extensive plantings, formal and kitchen gardens and a network of walks, monuments and viewpoints. Prince Albert set about planning this outstanding example of a 19th-century designed landscape as soon as he had purchased the estate. In 1852, he modelled his proposals in sand. The painter/landscape designer James Giles and the surveyor James F. Beattie helped with the layout and the firm of William Smith, architect of the castle, designed the terraces and parterres, assisted by the sculptor John Thomas. Terraces replaced the huge mounds of excavated earth in 1855, as the Royal apartments overlooking them were being completed. The following year, the 'flower plots' were planted and Queen Victoria noted in her Journal that the King of Prussia had presented an eagle fountain for 'the little garden on the west side'. It was Queen Mary's idea to recess the garden in the 1920s, in an attempt to counteract the biting winds. Until recently, as these photographs show, the immediate setting of the castle comprised large expanses of lawn, punctuated by two rose parterres.

In the south gardens, Queen Mary created her fountain garden in 1923–25. The Duke of Edinburgh developed the kitchen gardens in the 1950s and also laid out the water garden to the west.

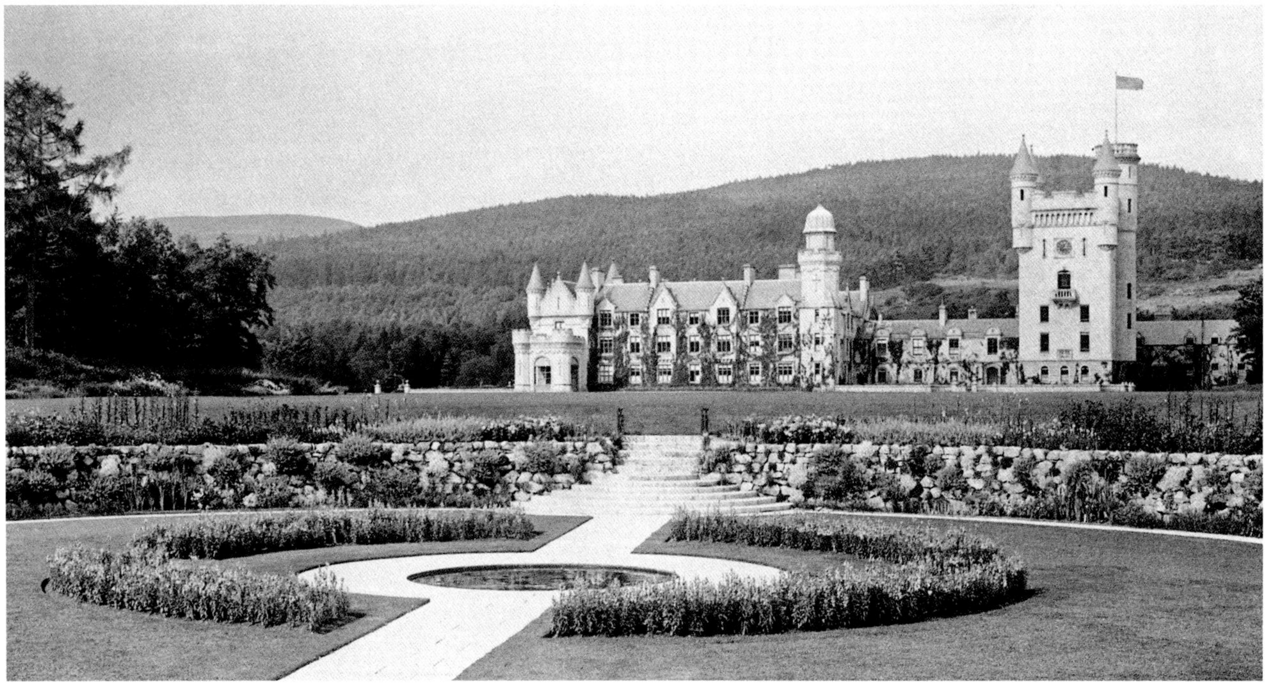

*left* A photograph from Volume 22 of Queen Mary's Album, showing the garden she created to the south of the castle, as it appeared around October–November 1924.

The setting of the castle as it appeared in Elizabeth II's day:

*right*  The Ballroom Lawn before 2023 (see p.59 for its appearance today). The photograph gives a good view of the ballroom, which is linked by a passage to the north side of the castle.

*below*  The Sunken Garden [left] and the rose garden that lies above it [right] on the private west side of the castle.

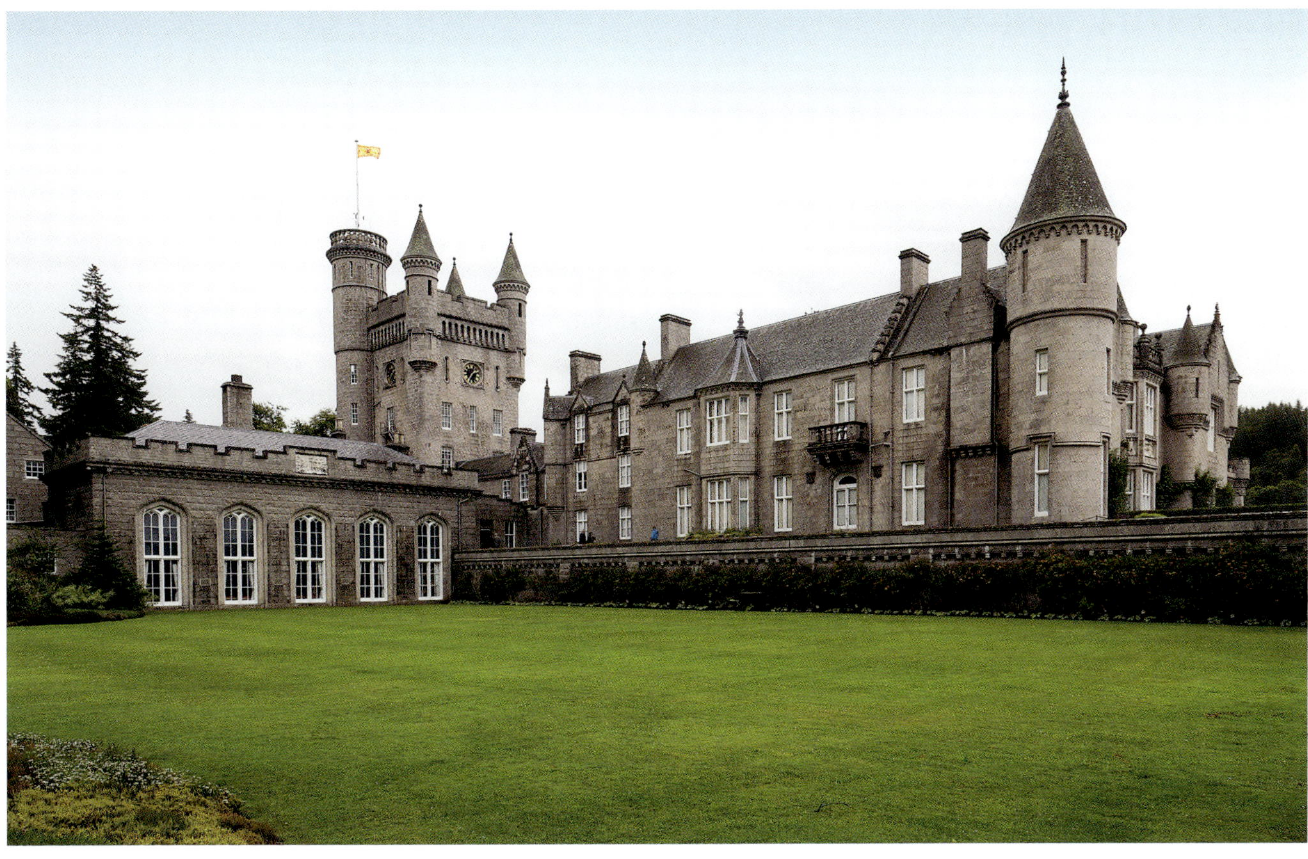

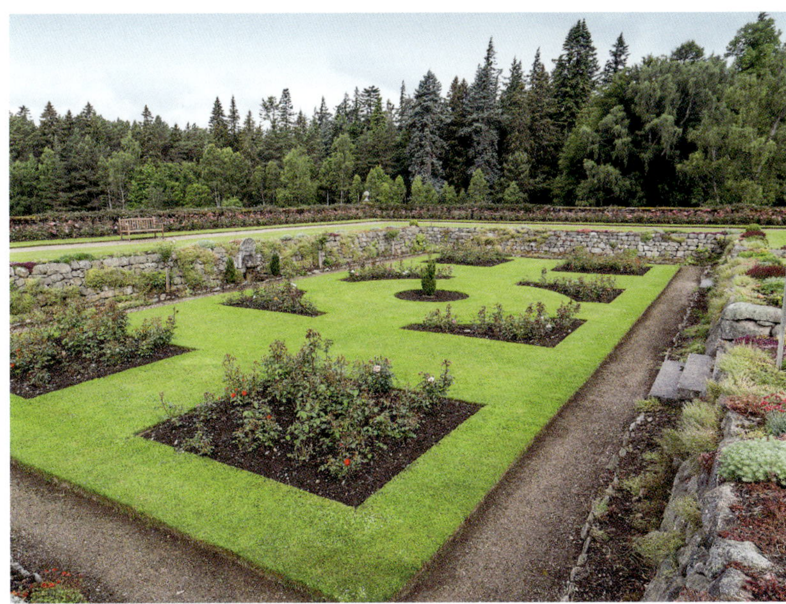

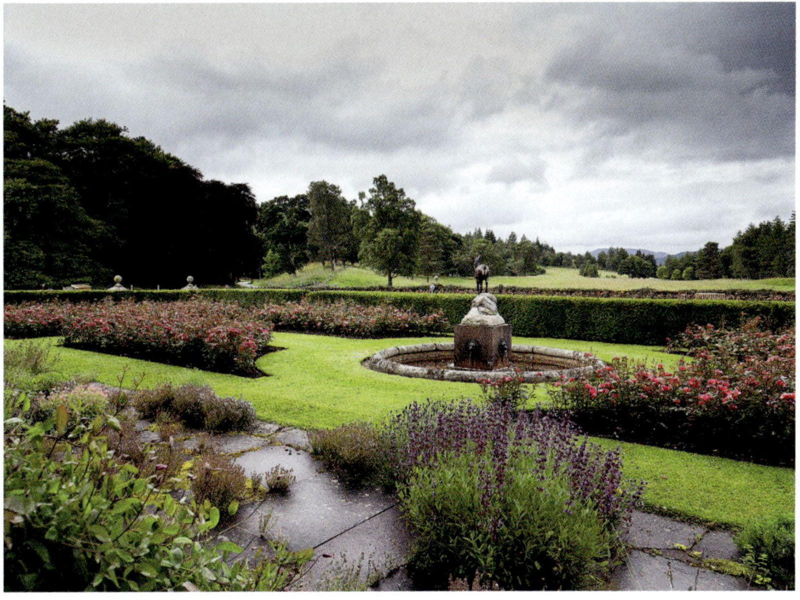

# The Renewal of the Gardens

The King's passion for gardening is renowned and it is this aspect of his ambitious programme to revitalise the castle and its setting that has had the greatest impact at Balmoral since he took over in 2022. Working with Kirsty Wilson, who leads a team of gardeners, His Majesty has transformed 45 acres, with gardens redesigned in his distinctive style and the kitchen and flower garden converted to a sustainable organic regime. Everything is done according to his long-held principles of harmony with Nature.

The existing gardens were tired and unsustainably managed when The King took them on, designed to flower in late summer, with little diversity or structure. Now they create a visual connection to the castle and are buzzing with pollinators. Unrelieved stretches of lawn provided, in effect, a blank canvas on to which His Majesty – a painter himself – could introduce colour, texture and shape. Edges have now been softened with shrubs, trees chosen for autumnal tints and a myriad spring bulbs.

The influence of other gardens The King has transformed is strong, in particular Birkhall, where he has learnt what works best in this climate. Like them, Balmoral reflects his traditional British style: the love of topiary – yew arches, box buttresses and whimsical shapes – herbaceous borders, spring bulbs, fragrant blooms and, of course, majestic trees. His commitment to craftsmanship is also evident, with a dovecot, benches and other structures made using traditional materials and skills.



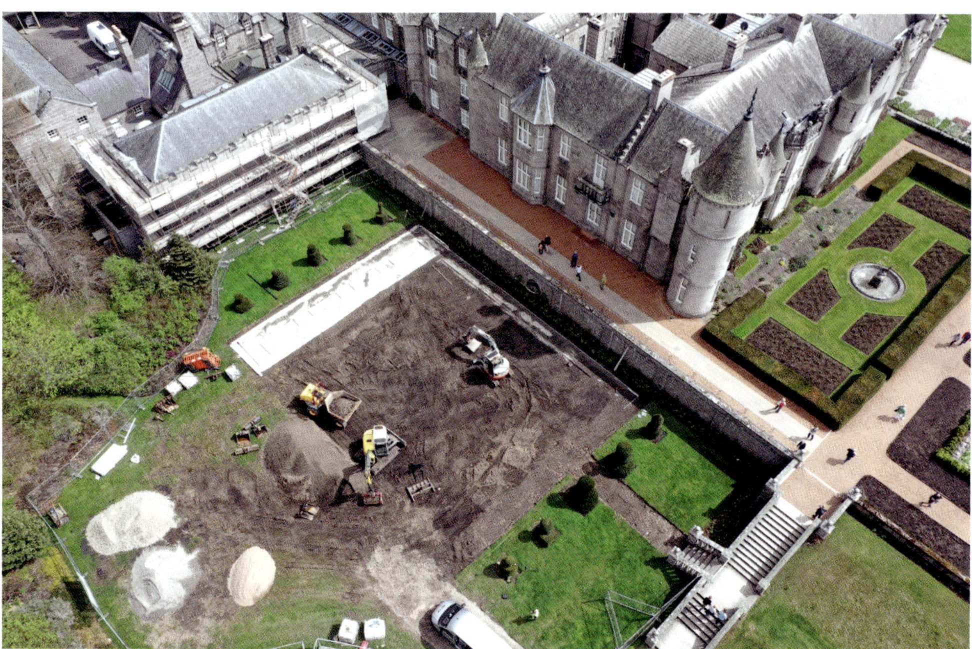

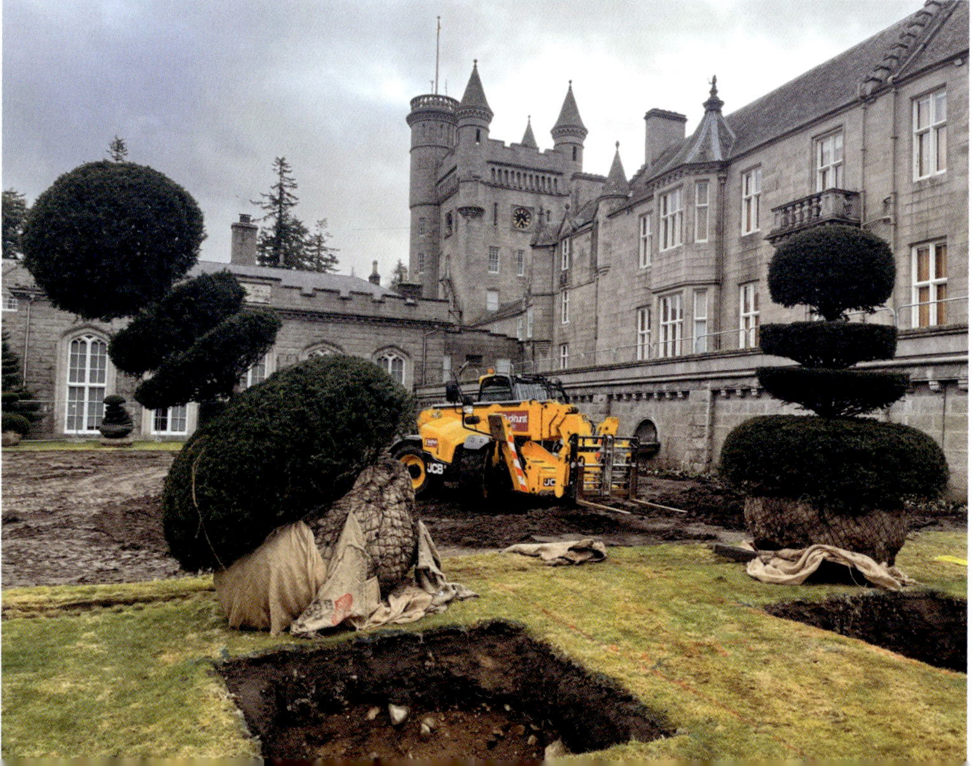

*left above and below*
Excavation works and
installation of topiary on the
Ballroom Lawn in 2024, to
create and build the Celtic
Maze.

*top right*  Work in progress
in Queen Mary's Garden
in autumn 2023, with
prepared beds awaiting
the installation of the yew
'puddings' around the old
fountain, which has now
been replaced.

*below right*  Works in
progress in the newly
designed Sunken Garden on
the west side of the castle,
2024.

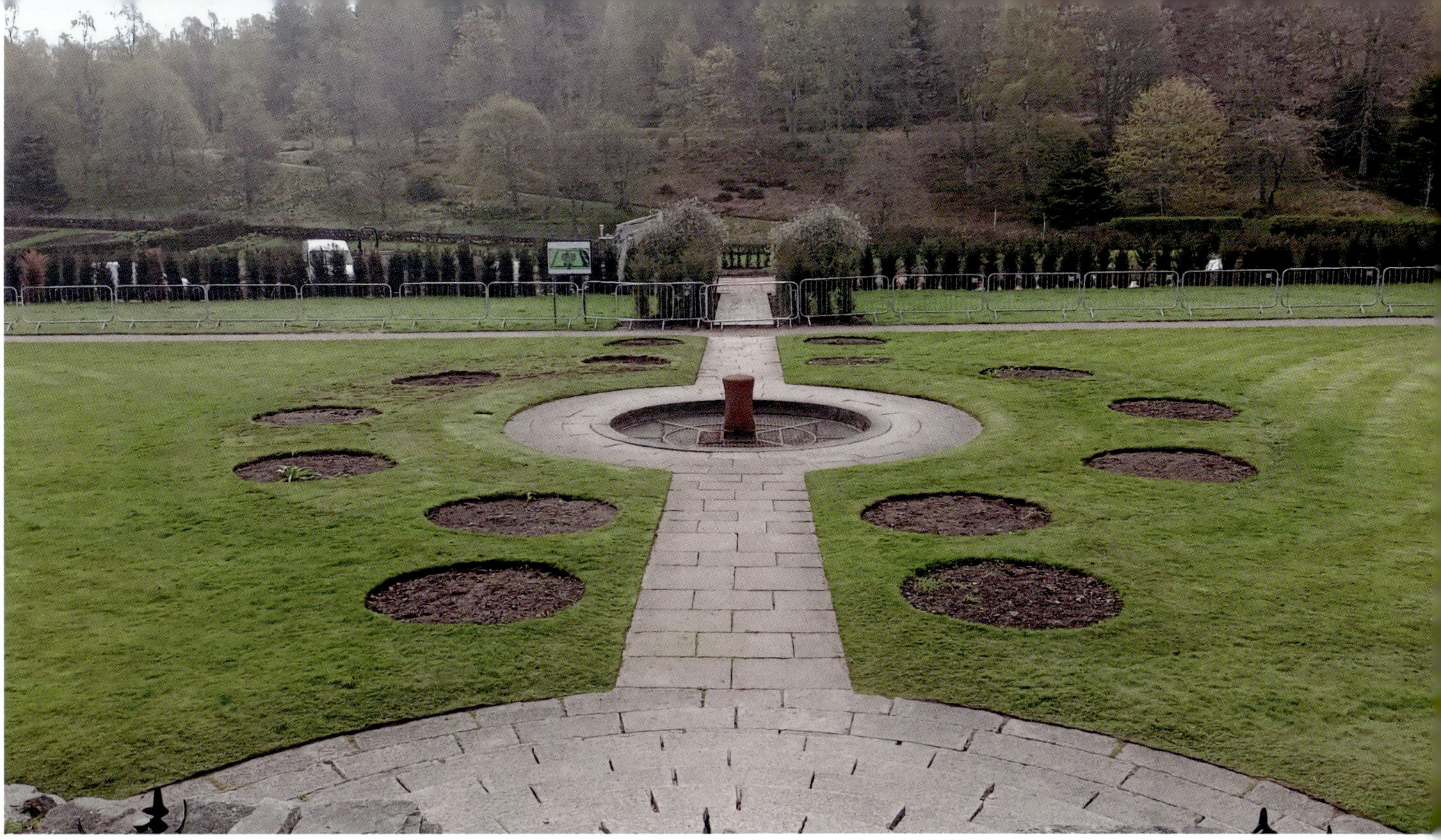

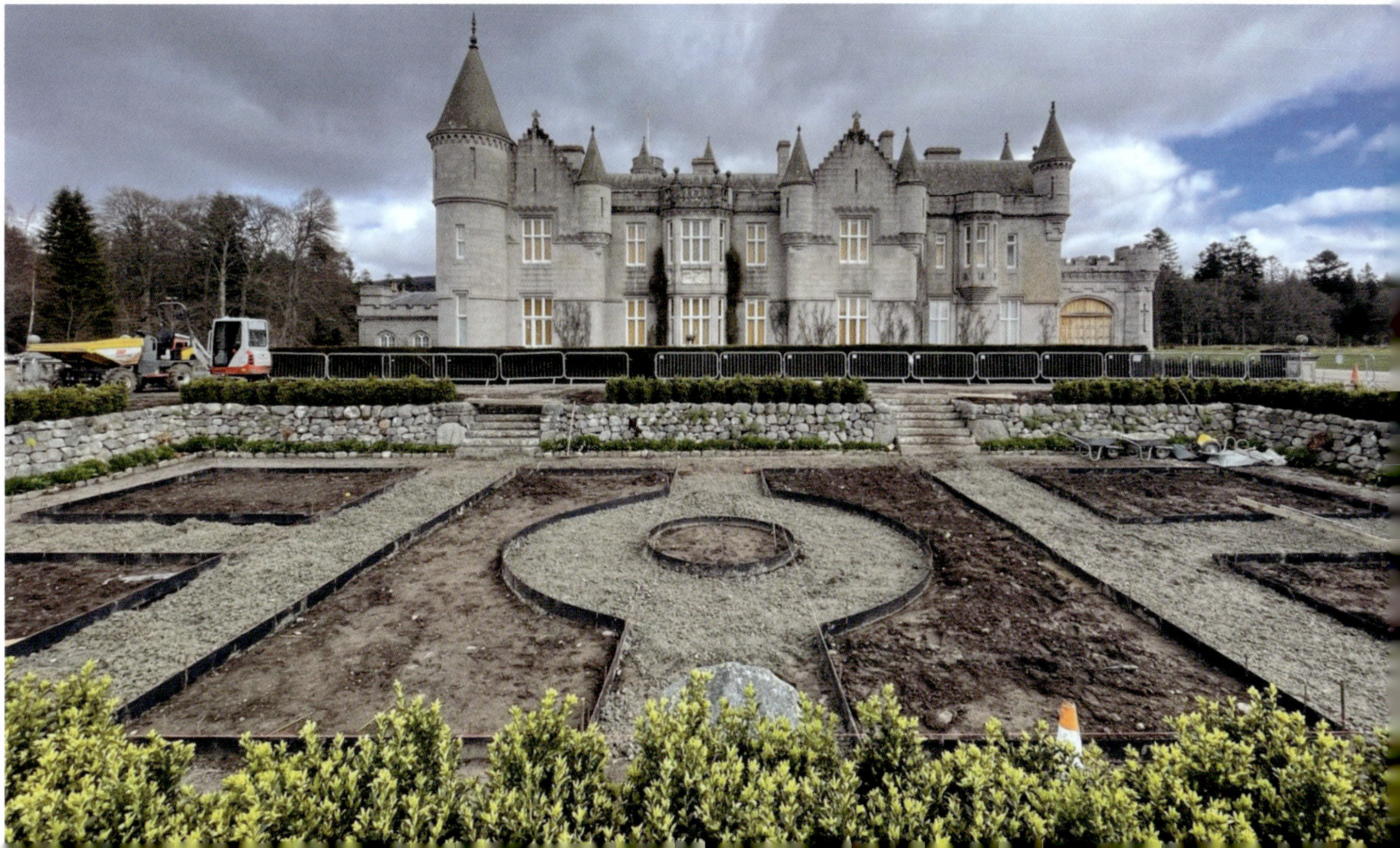

# The Sunken Garden

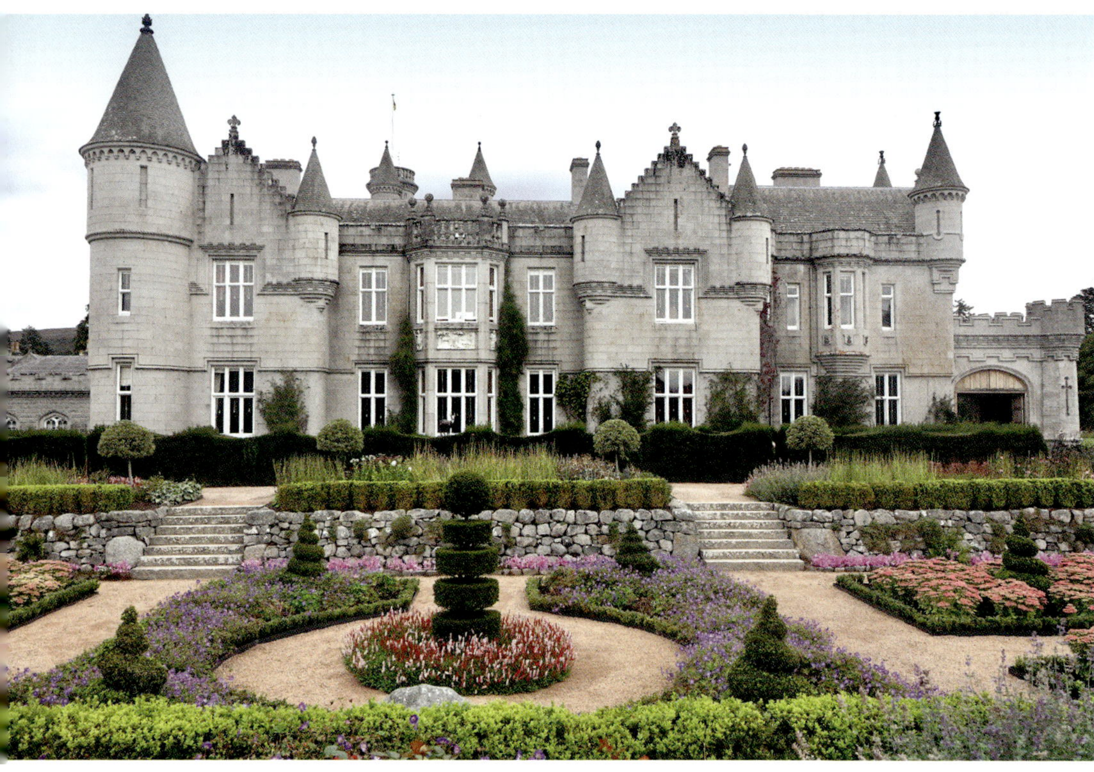

Until 2024, Queen Mary's creation on the castle's exposed west side was a classic late-summer rose garden, planted to flower when the Royal Family was in residence. The King has completely transformed it, replacing the rose beds with a traditional box parterre. This is framed by crow-stepped yew hedges and planted with herbaceous perennials in soft pinks and purples, and with 'Olivia Rose Austin'. Spring and autumn bulbs fill beds and surrounding borders ornamented with box swirls and lollipops of variegated holly. Autumn-flowering sedums provide late colour and food for pollinators and the topiary gives structure.

*above*  The Sunken Garden enhances the transitory space between indoors and outdoors and draws the eye out into the wider borrowed landscape.

*right*  The parterre and borders are filled with pollinator-friendly plants such as nepeta, salvia, aster, achillea, paeonia in a palette of pinks and purples. The stone wall's box coping was modelled on one at Birkhall.

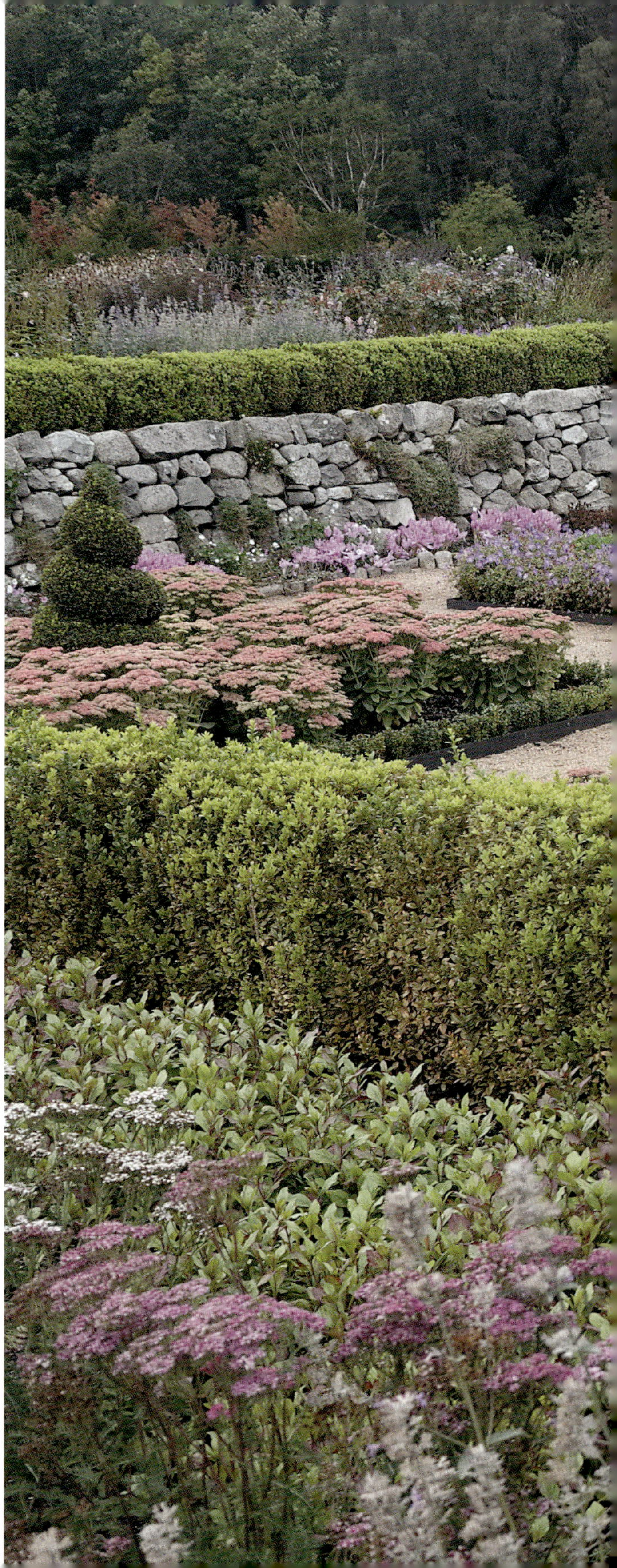

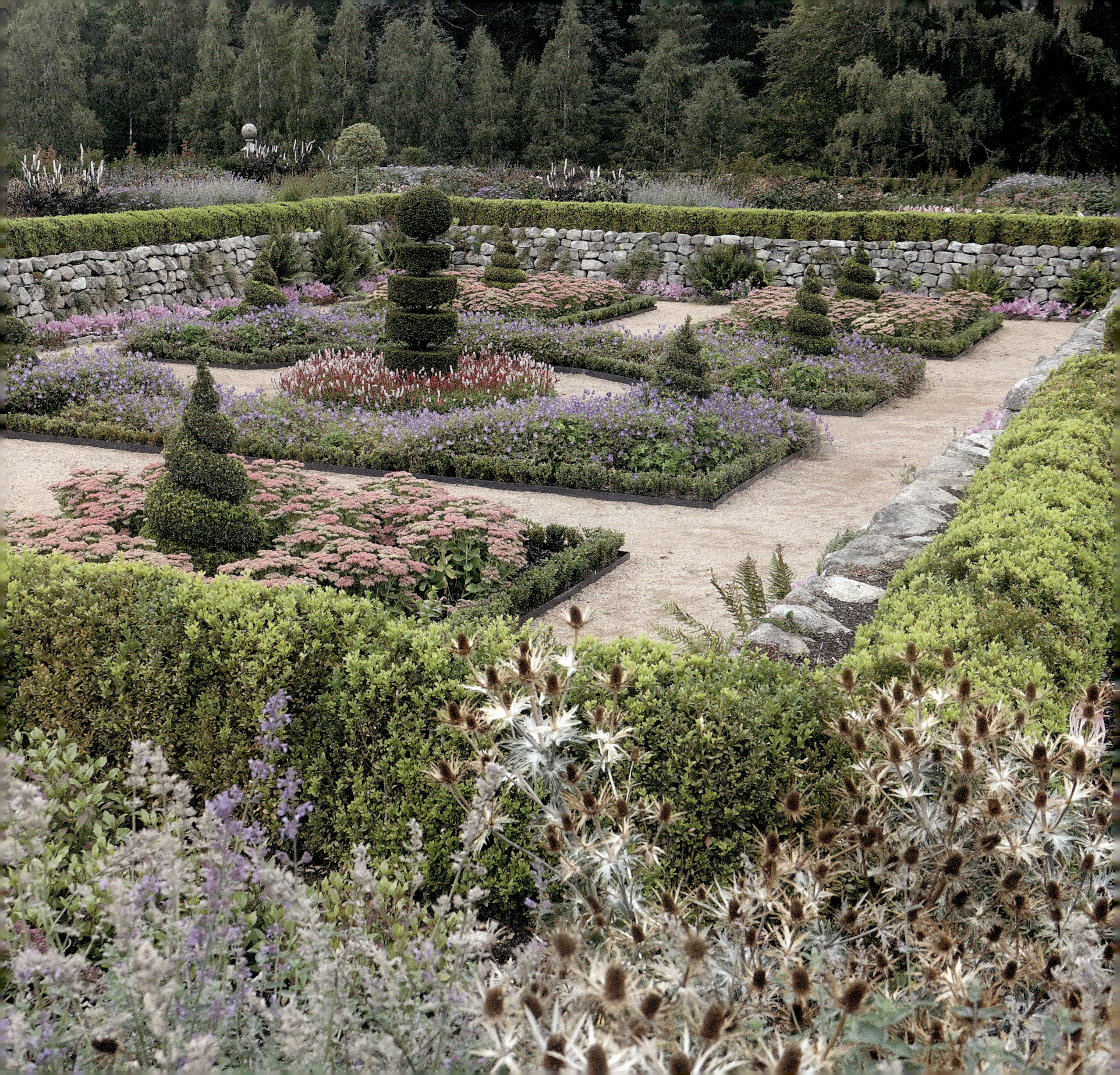

# The Celtic Ballroom Maze

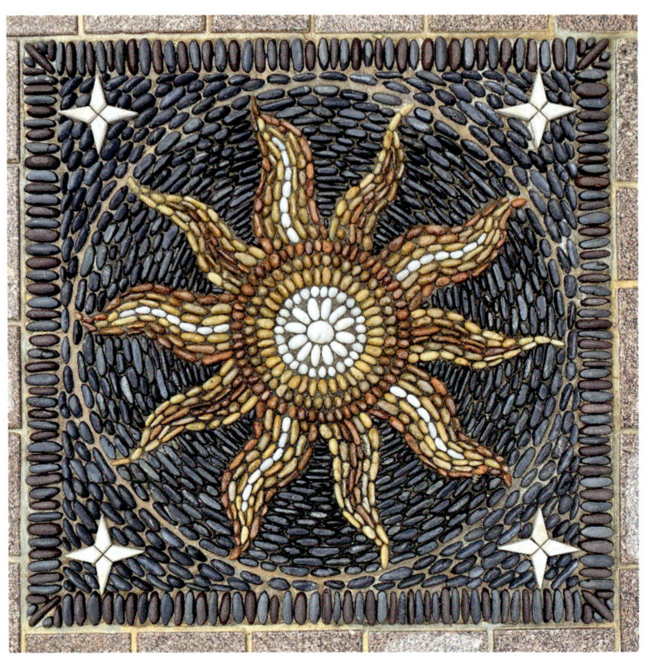

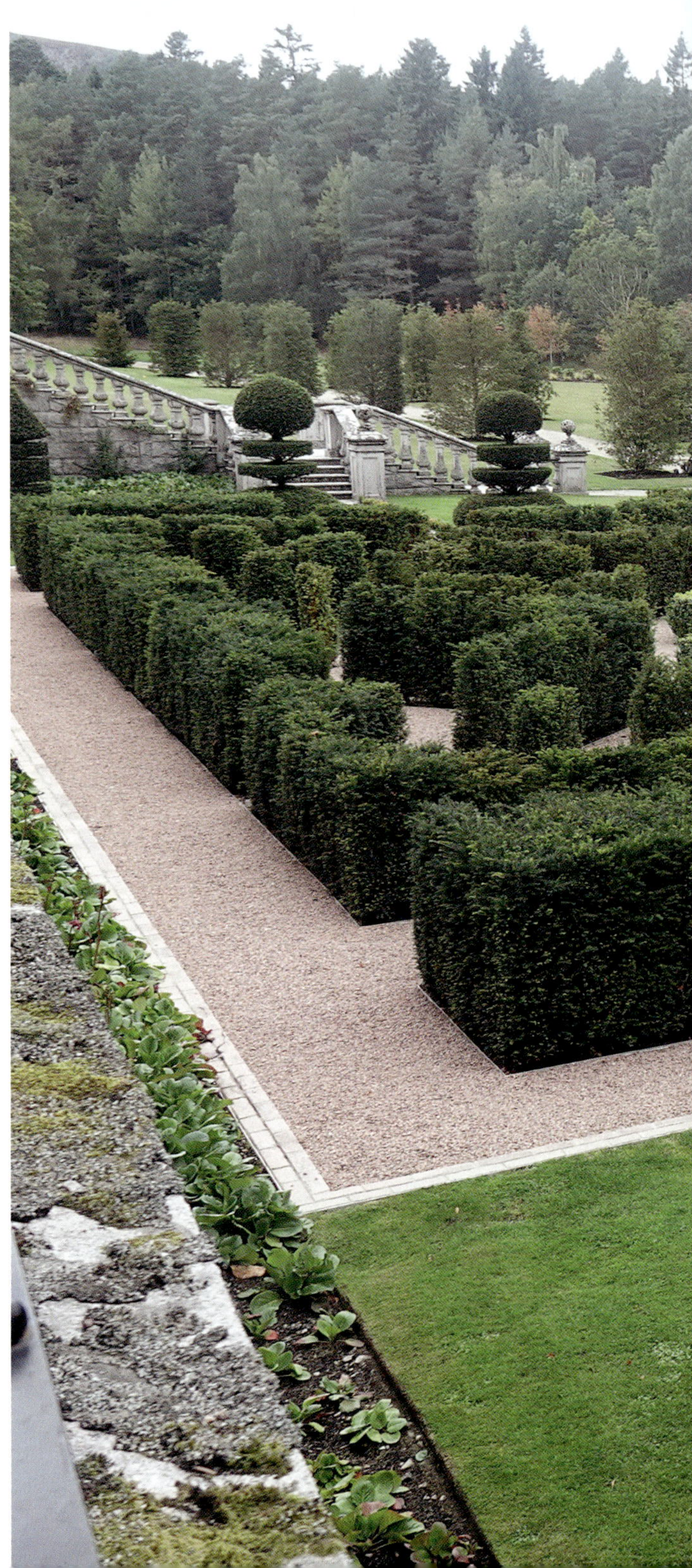

*left*  One of four pebble mosaics inset within the maze. Designed by Maggy Howarth Studios, they feature a sun (seen here), moon, star and compass.

*right*  Harmony amidst complexity: the Celtic Ballroom Maze was created in 2024 to enhance the flat ground between the north front of the castle and the Dee. The lawns leading to the river are fringed with new plantings, including rhododendrons, acers, sorbus, heathers and hydrangeas.

Formerly a dull expanse of grass, the Ballroom Lawn has given way to an intricate maze that reflects His Majesty's interest in geometric pattern and the symbolism of labyrinths. It was designed by Dr Khaled Azzam and his students at The King's Foundation School of Traditional Arts in the form of a Celtic knot, inspired by the motifs decorating 9th-century illuminated man-uscripts and carved Pictish stones. Integrated into the yew knot are four open squares paved with cosmic mosaics and four squares of box containing fanciful swirls. The latter, together with the surrounding topiary, adds a charac-teristic air of caprice, while the design of the pebble mosaic path hints at His Majesty's love of Islamic gardens.

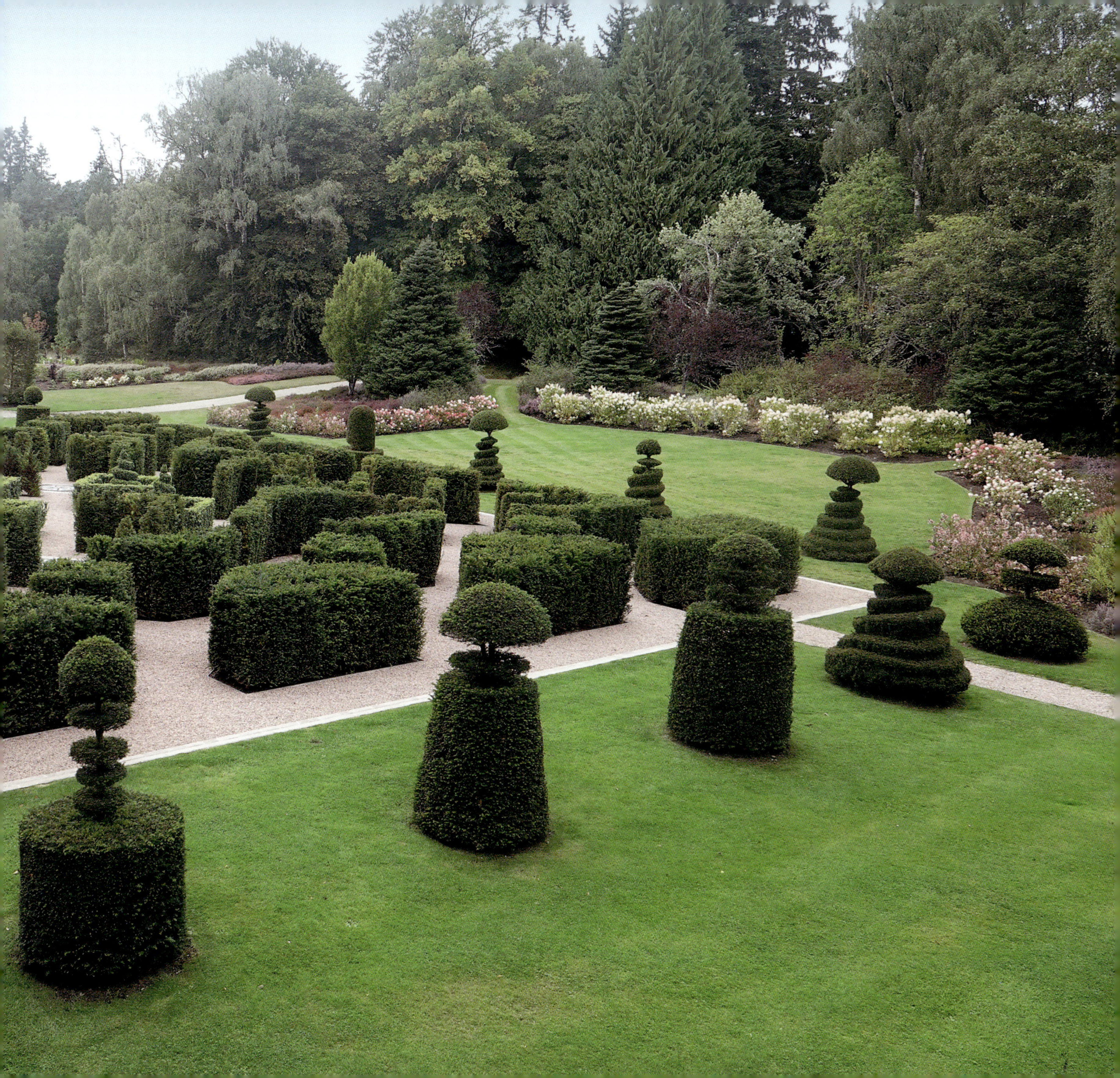

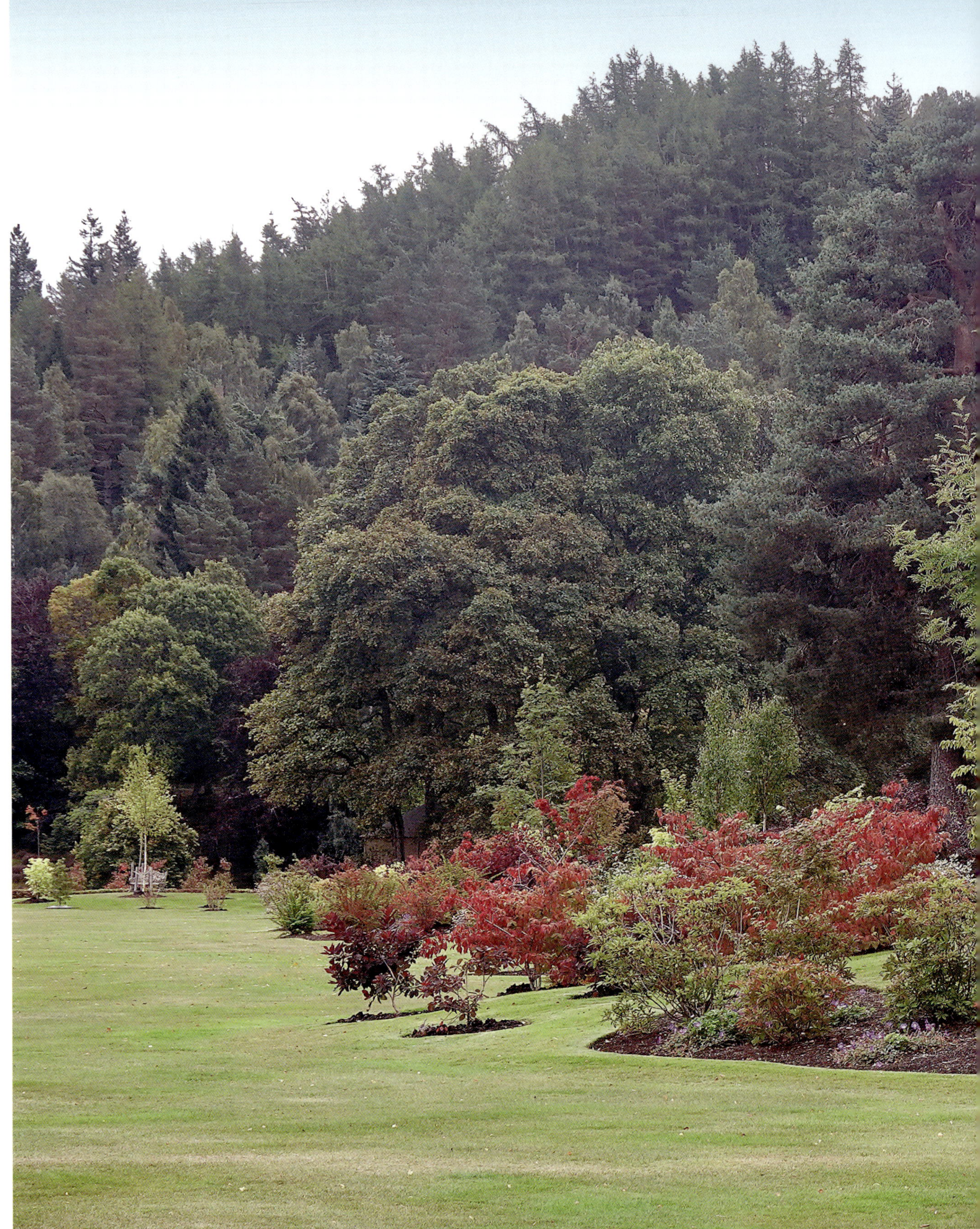

*right* Some of the new plantings designed to soften the edges of the south lawn and add spring and autumn interest. They include shrubs and herbaceous flowers, such as rhododendron, hydrangea, cotinus (smoke bush) and aronia (chokeberry), underplanted with spring bulbs, and deciduous trees such as acer, birch, cornus and sorbus.

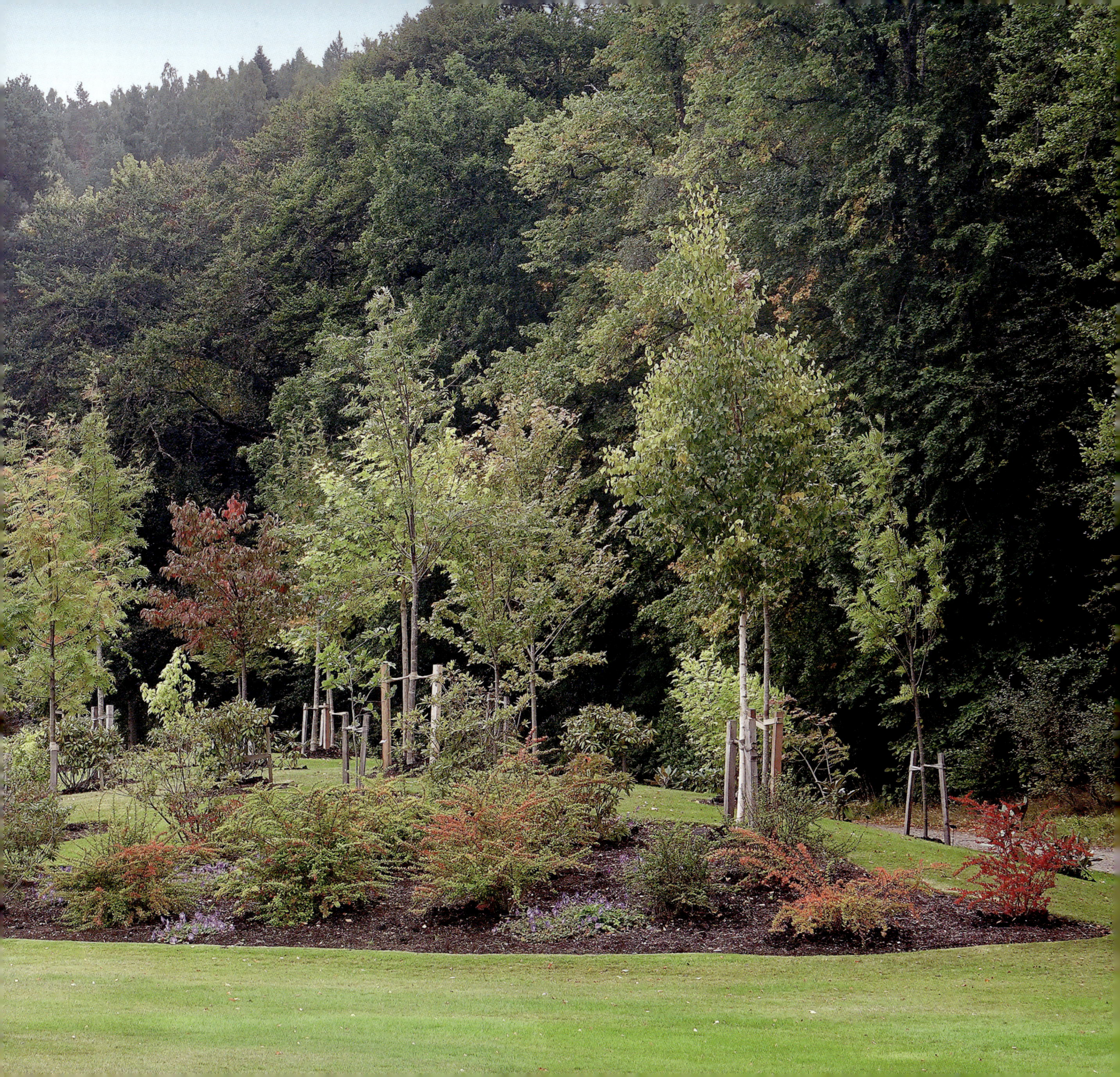

# Queen Mary's Garden

The fountain garden, created by Queen Mary in 1923–25, forms a bell-shaped enclosure at the far end of the south lawn. It is entered through delightful wrought-iron gates that were remodelled in 2023 to celebrate their centenary and to herald the re-creation of the garden. His Majesty has done away with old-fashioned summer bedding and introduced his favourite elements of topiary and axial vistas to provide structure and geometrical form. Along the enclosing wall, a low beech hedge now emphasises the wide curve and adds shelter to the garden, which is set into a gentle slope. The beech leaves provide winter colour, as does the terrace skirting the wall, which is planted with delicate alpines that thrive all year round in the Highland climate, at an altitude of nearly 1,000 feet.

Curved steps lead down on to a broad, stone-paved path that links the gates, via two yew arches and more steps, to the Thistle Maze and cylindrical dovecot. The path is punctuated by a circular basin with a fountain in the form of a pierced marble disc, surrounded by spherical yew 'puddings'. The fountain was a gift from the musician Sting.

Replacing the former annual beds, an avenue of cherry trees runs horizontally across the garden. Hardy *Prunus sargentii* was chosen because it performs so well up here and provides spectacular seasonal displays, from rosy-pink blossom to fiery autumn shades.

*right* The gate was remodelled by local blacksmith Craig Monteith of The Crooked Shed. The upper register is the 1923 original, monogrammed GR (George Rex) and MR (Mary Regina). The lower register bears the letters CR (Charles Rex) and CR (Camilla Regina), their contrasting, lighter fonts suited to the oak-leaf decoration that entwines the gilded monograms.



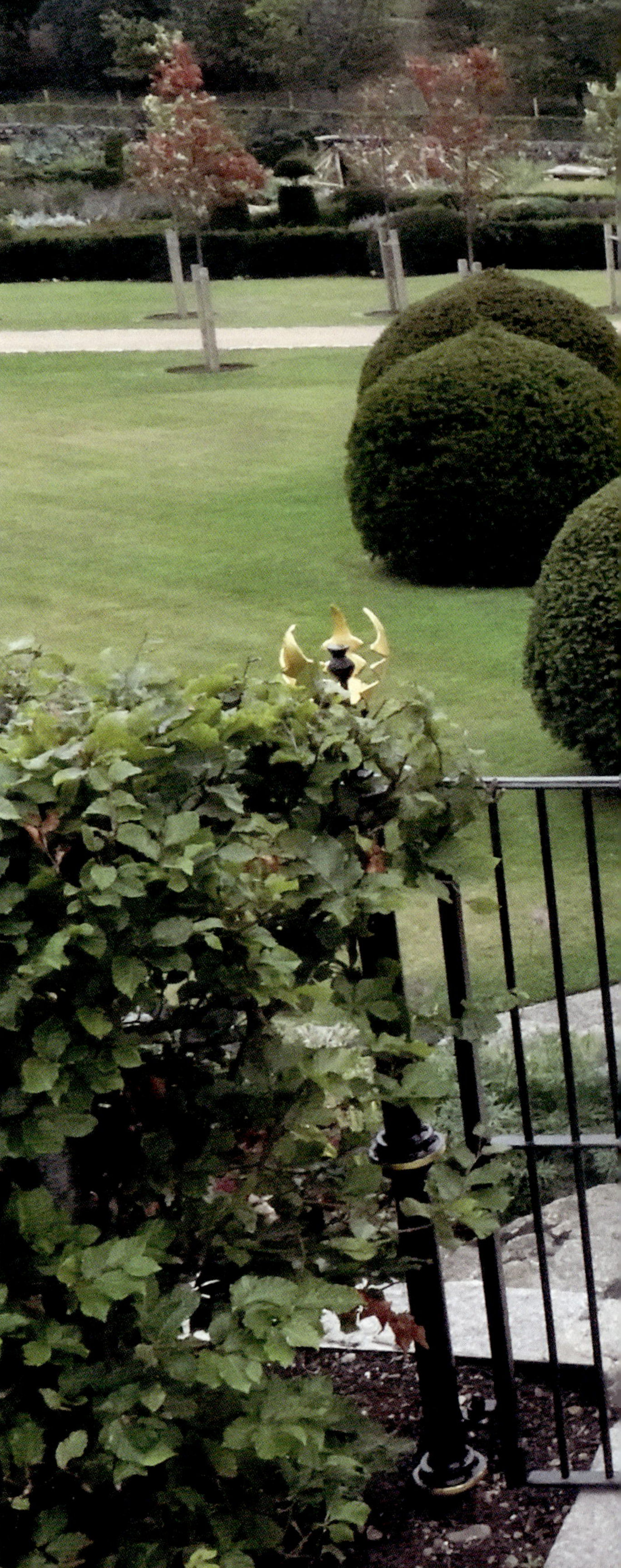

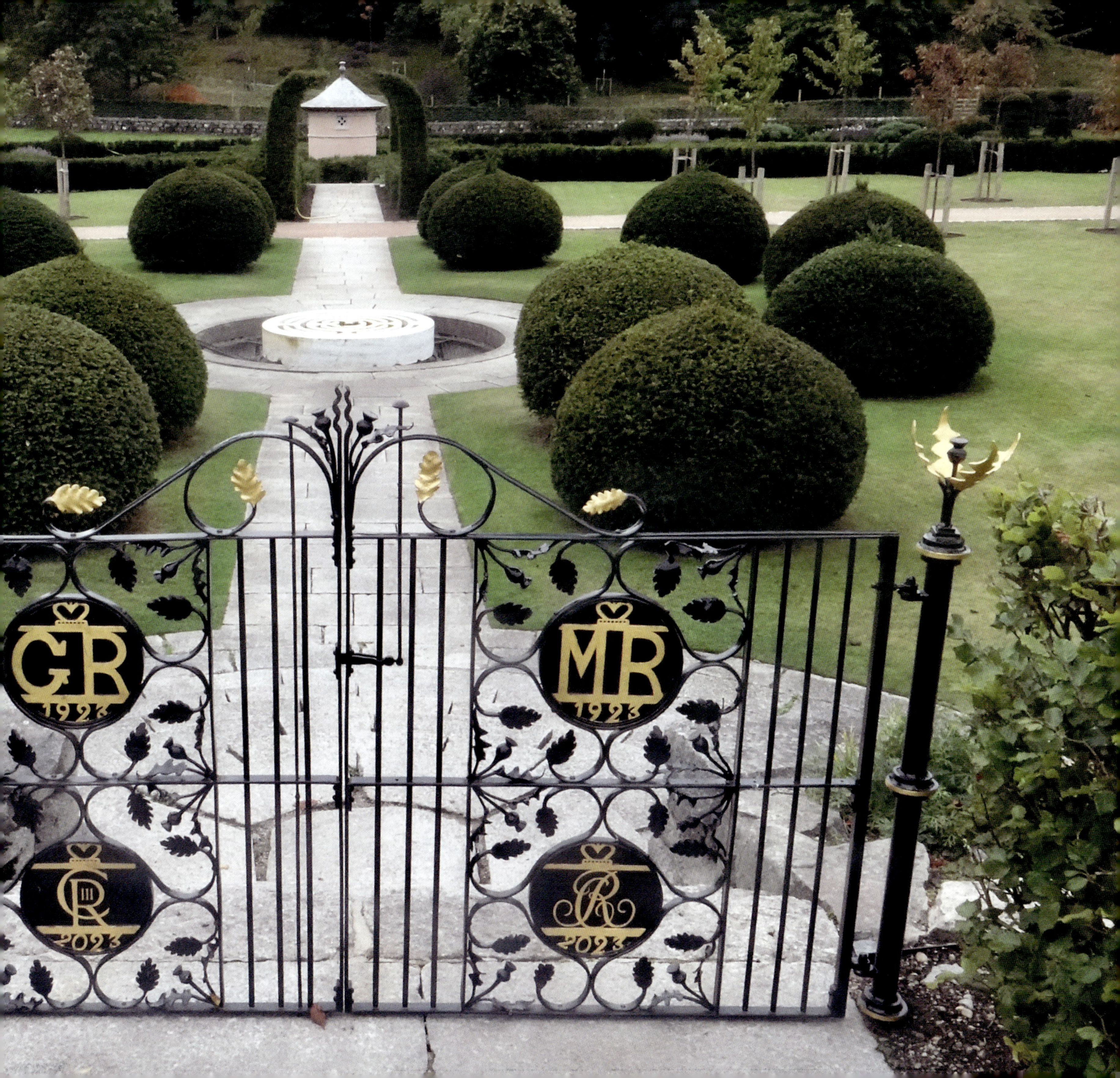

# The Thistle Maze

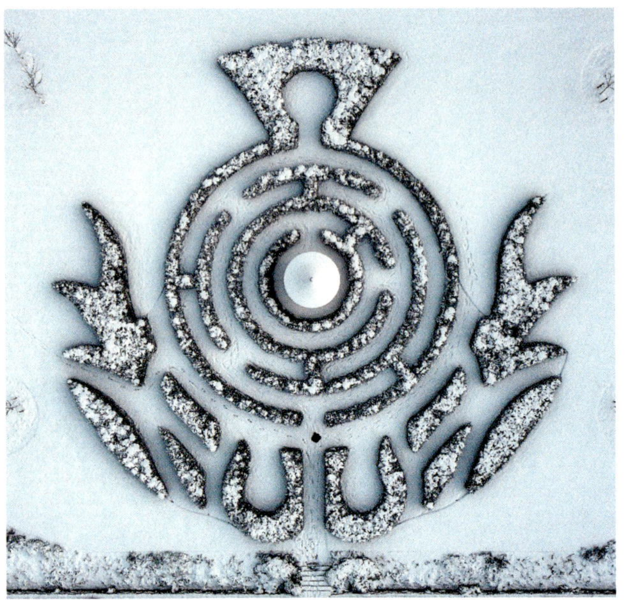

His Majesty's vision, realised with Head of Gardens Kirsty Wilson, was to create a yew maze representing the national flower of Scotland. Thistles are a recurring theme at Balmoral, both in the interior and exterior decoration of the castle (thistle finials surmount some turrets), and in the gardens, such as the corner herbaceous beds around the maze.

The dovecot reflects The King's love of ornamental garden structures and his commitment to Arts & Crafts principles. Designed by Keith Ross, it was constructed by local stone masons and estate workers, using natural materials. Along two sides of the garden, a sorbus lawn and a 'hot' border counterbalance the evergreen with autumnal berries and sedums, and with rudbeckia, echinacea, achillea, crocosmia and geum.

*left* An aerial view of the Thistle Maze taken in the winter of 2025. The centre of the flowerhead is the circular roof of the dovecot, which is topped with a thistle finial.

*right* The Thistle Maze, looking north to Queen Mary's Garden, with its yew 'puddings' and newly – planted cherry avenue. The ornamental dovecot by Keith Ross of Dovecot Architecture and Design is lime rendered with a cedar-shingle roof. On the right is Elizabeth II's Jubilee Conservatory.

*following pages* View from the Thistle Maze over Queen Mary's Garden to the south front of the castle, which is seen against the backdrop of Creag Mhòr across the Dee. Between the towers, the 1859 Tower Garden has recently been redesigned with box and yew structures around its fountain (not visible).

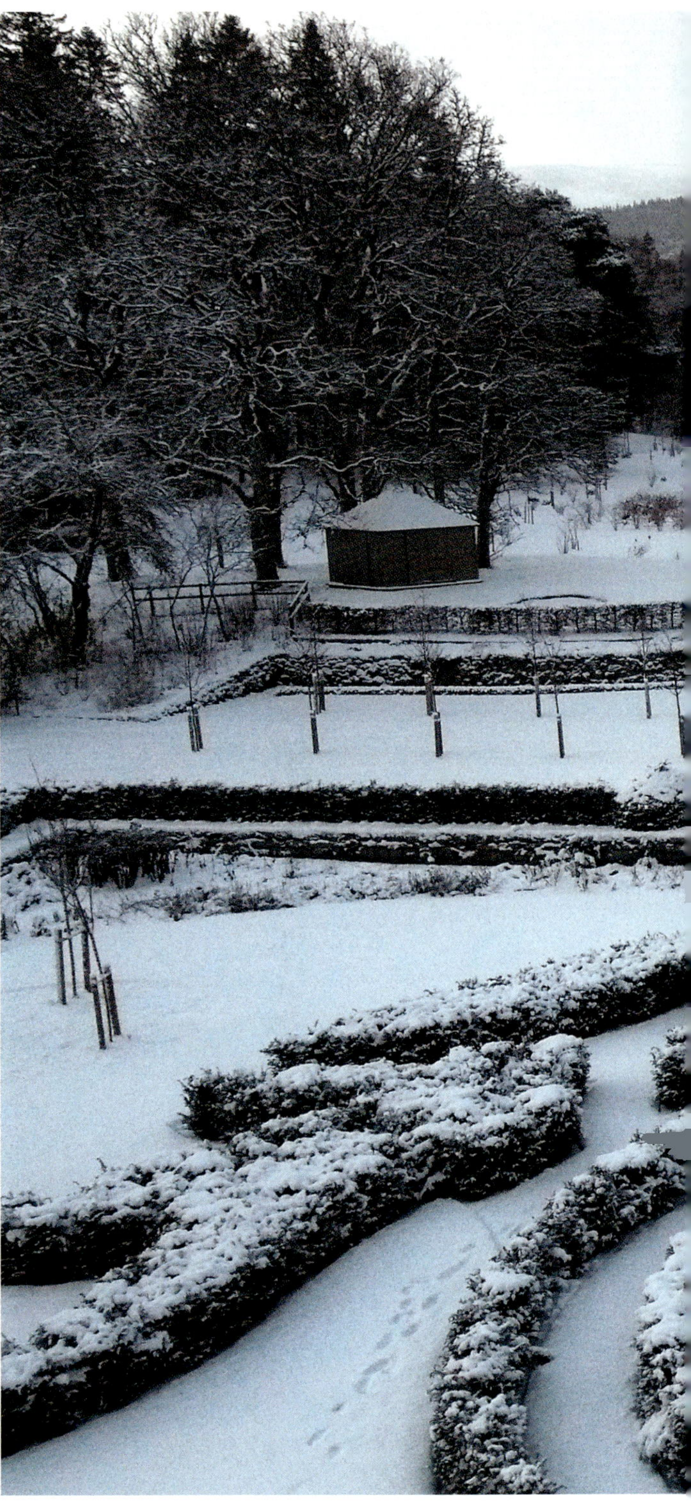

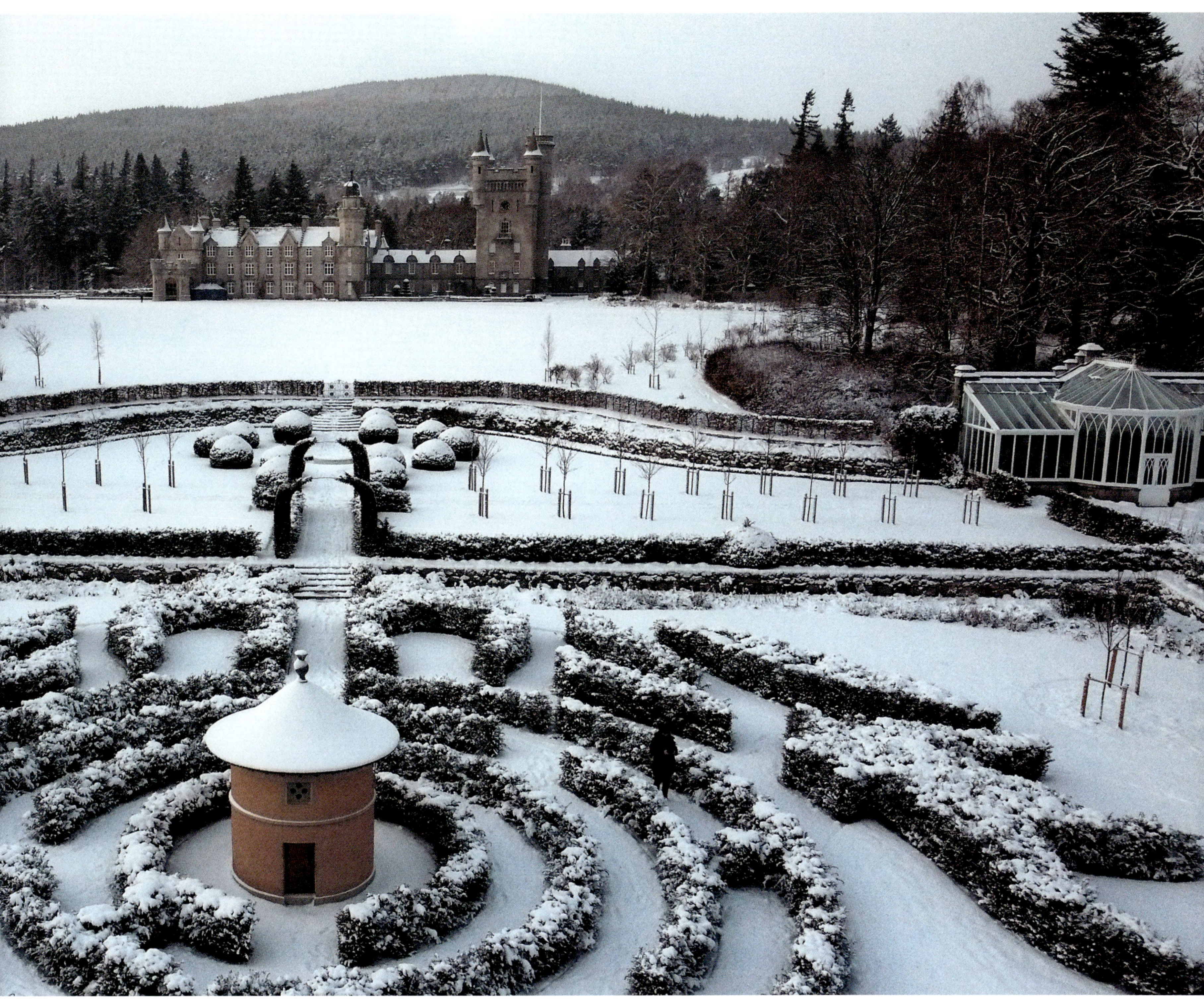

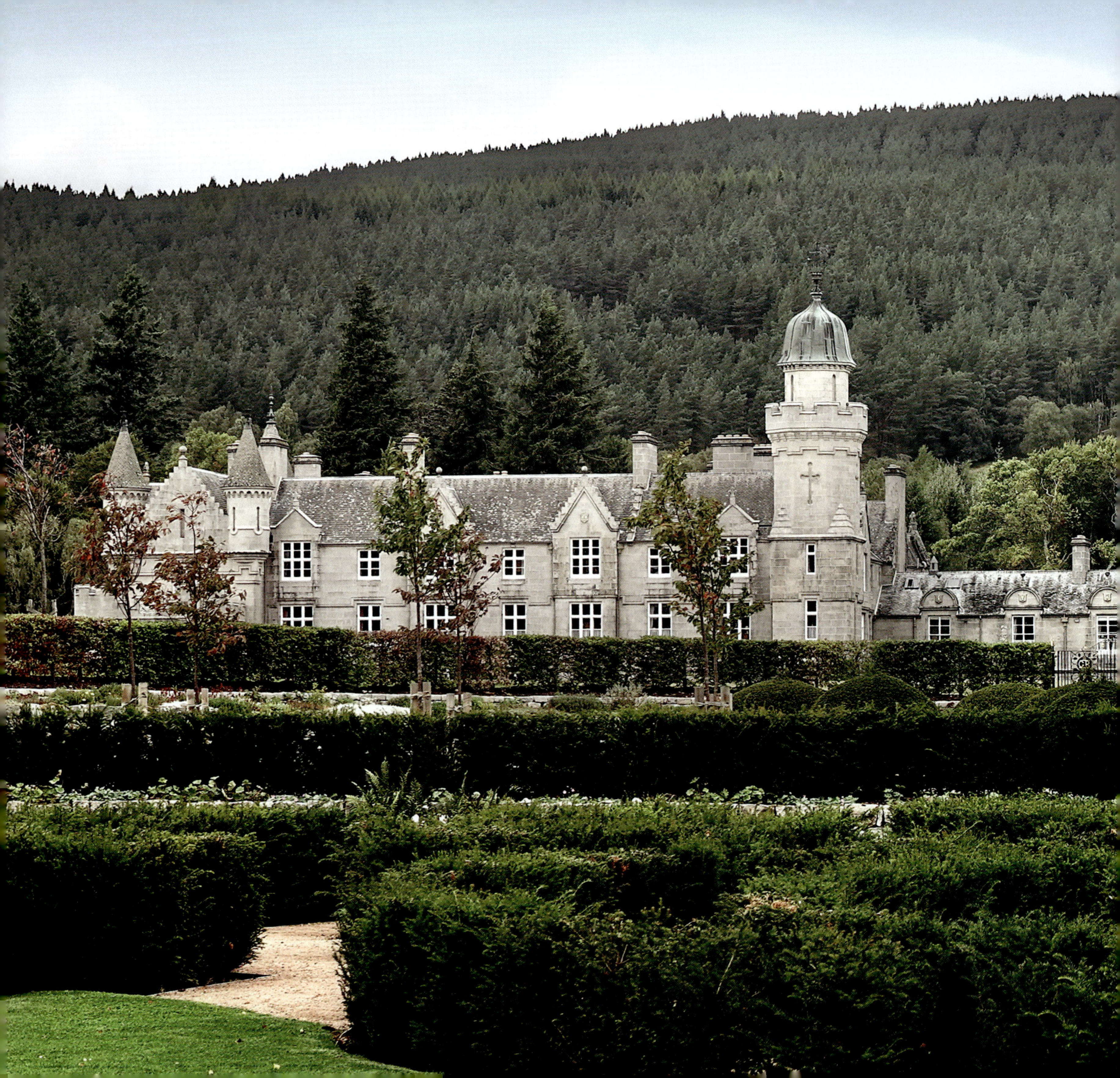

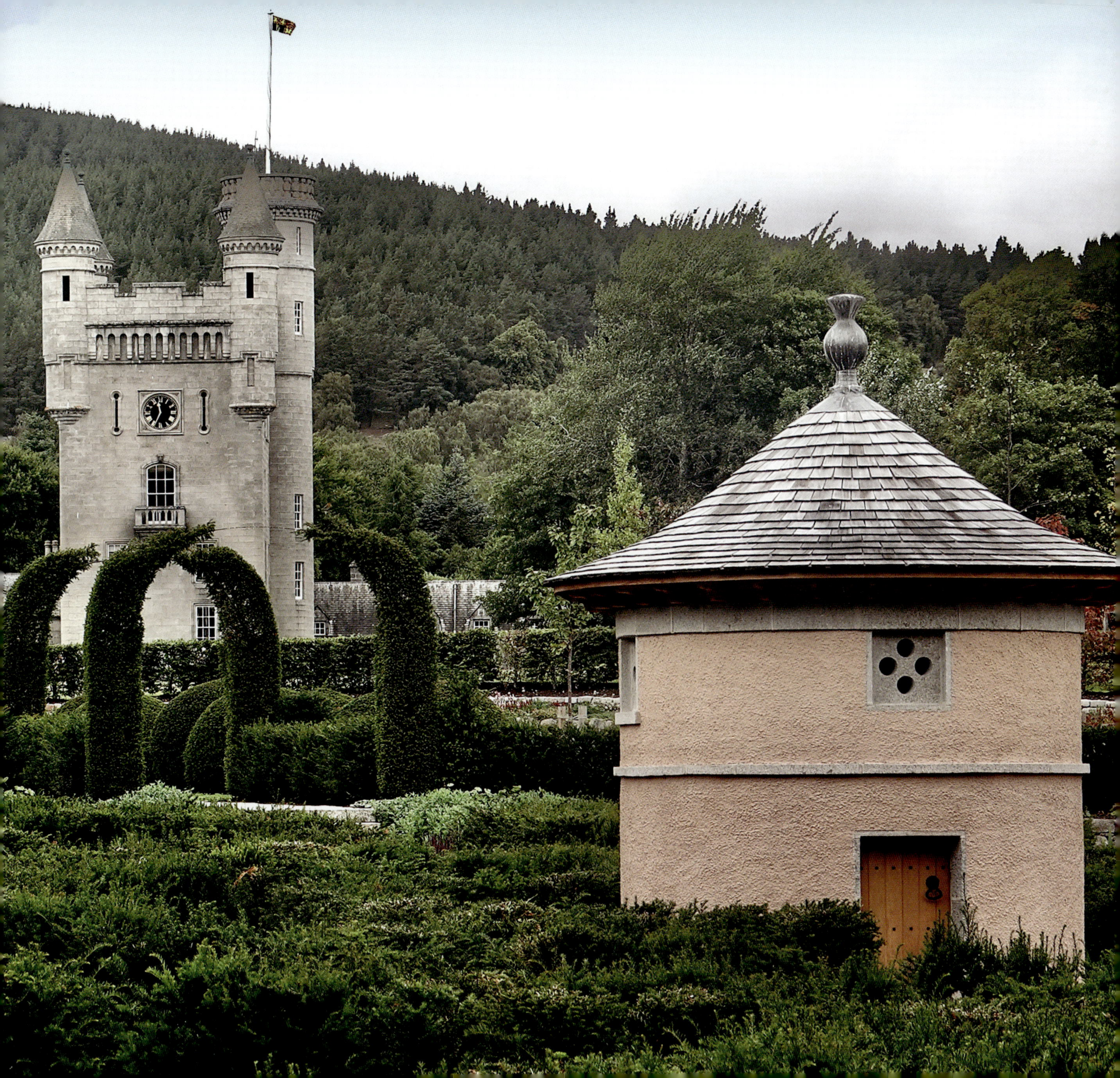

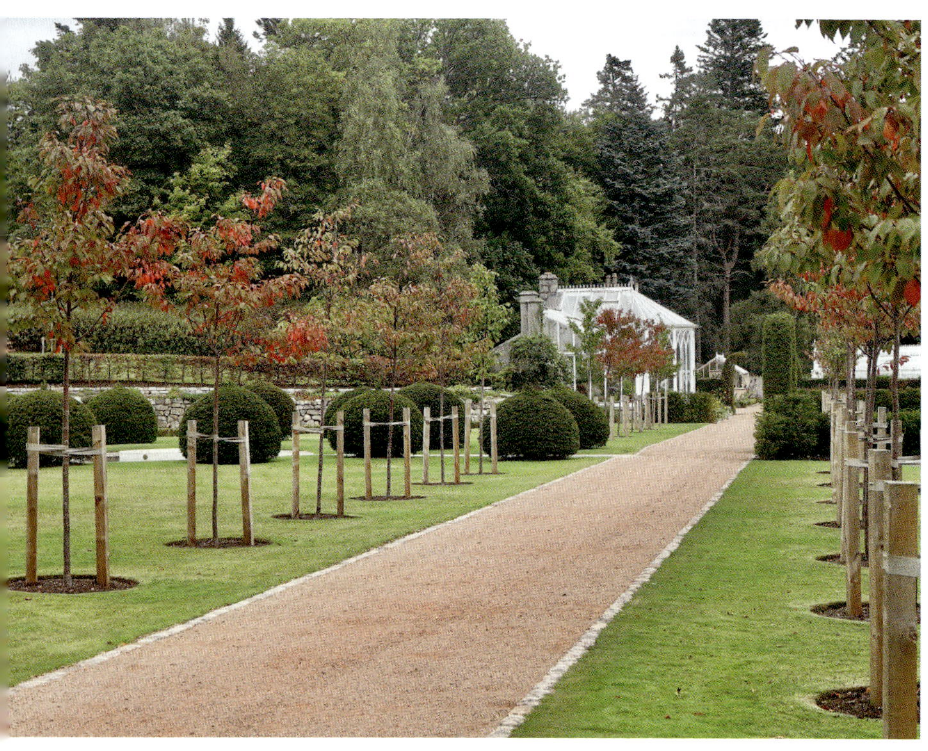 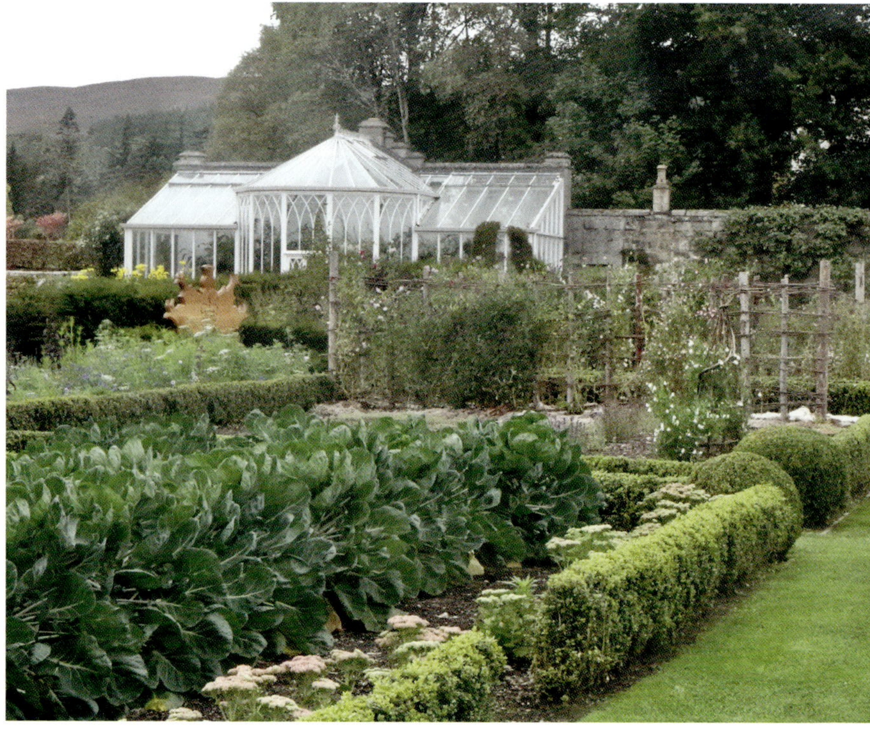

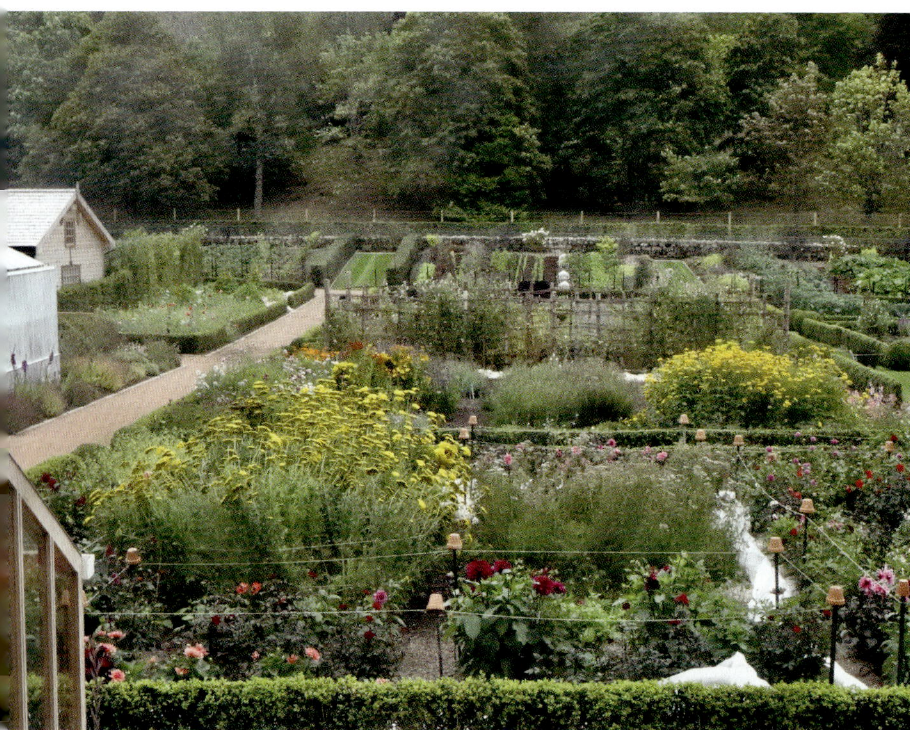 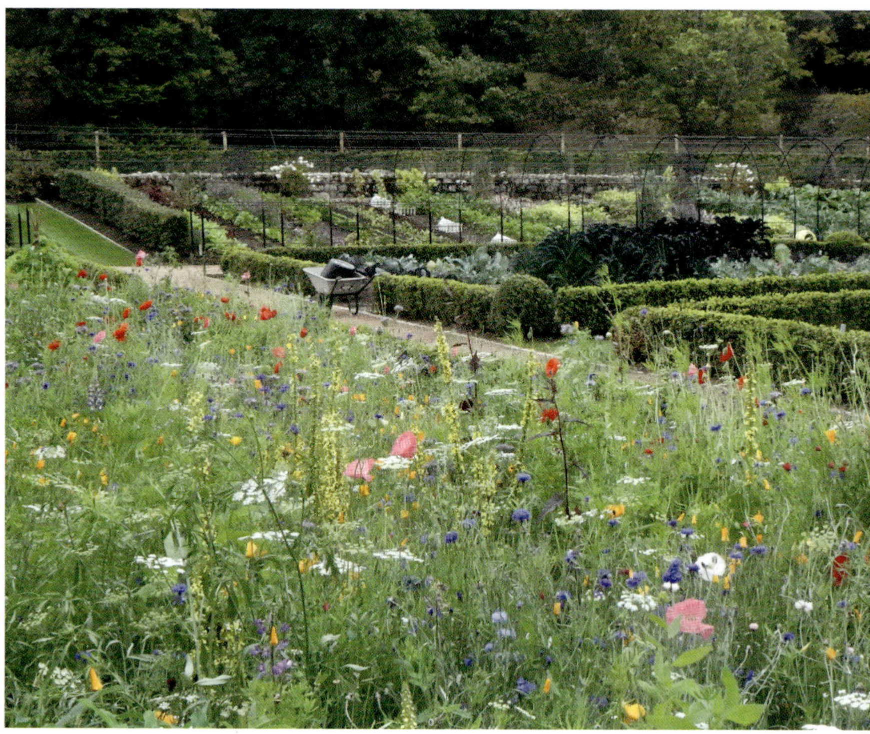

# The Kitchen Garden and Glasshouses

In the mountain fastness of the Dee Valley, July is the only guaranteed frost-free month and the soil is poor, so great care goes into preparing beds, bringing on seedlings in the glass houses and planting them out to be at maximum production when the Royal Family is in residence.

A nursery was 'trenched, laid-out, fenced, and filled with plants' in 1881. Today, it produces hundreds of vegetables, soft and orchard fruits, and more exotic ones, such as figs and peaches. Dating from 1876, the cut-flower garden provides the castle with fresh blooms for daily arrangements. House plants are a big thing too, particularly scented pelargoniums and jasmine. Everything is organically composted and grown using no chemicals or pesticides.

*opposite, clockwise from top left*

The cherry avenue of *Prunus sargentii* bisecting Queen Mary's Garden.

The Jubilee Conservatory from the vegetable beds.

Annual meadow mix, with pumpkins and brassicas in the box-lined beds and the plum tunnel in the distance.

The cut-flower garden with the kitchen garden beyond, divided by a sweet-pea avenue with fences of woven willow.

*right*  The Jubilee Conservatory was given to the late Queen by her staff for her Golden Jubilee in 2002. Filled with traditional house plants, such as pelargonium, jasmine, streptocarpus, fuchsia and schizanthus, it is also used for themed flower displays. The inscription over the door reads: 'One is nearer God's heart in a garden than anywhere else on earth.'

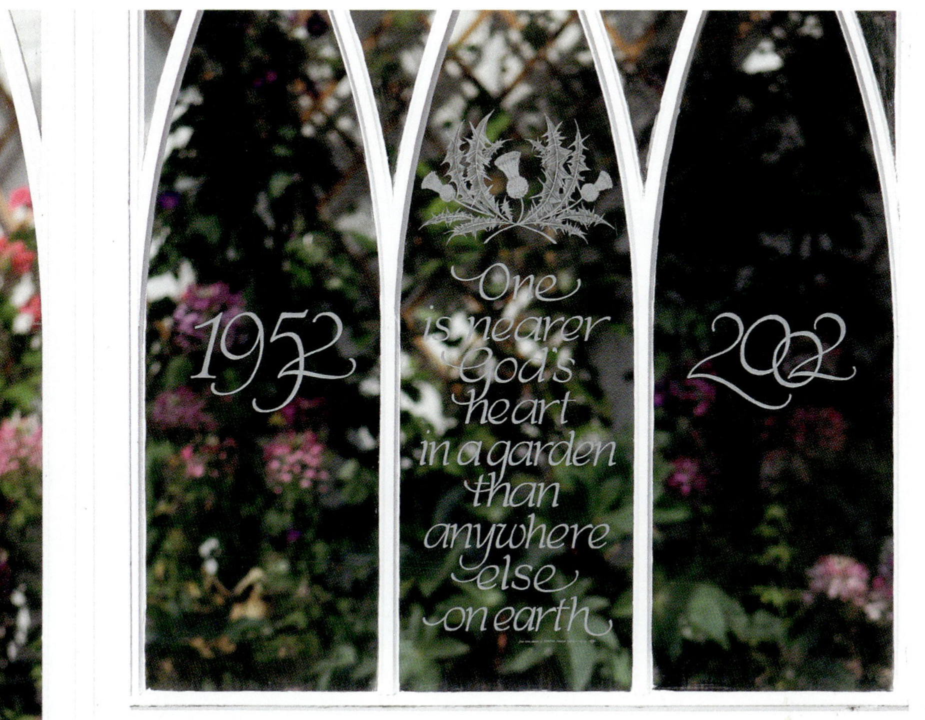


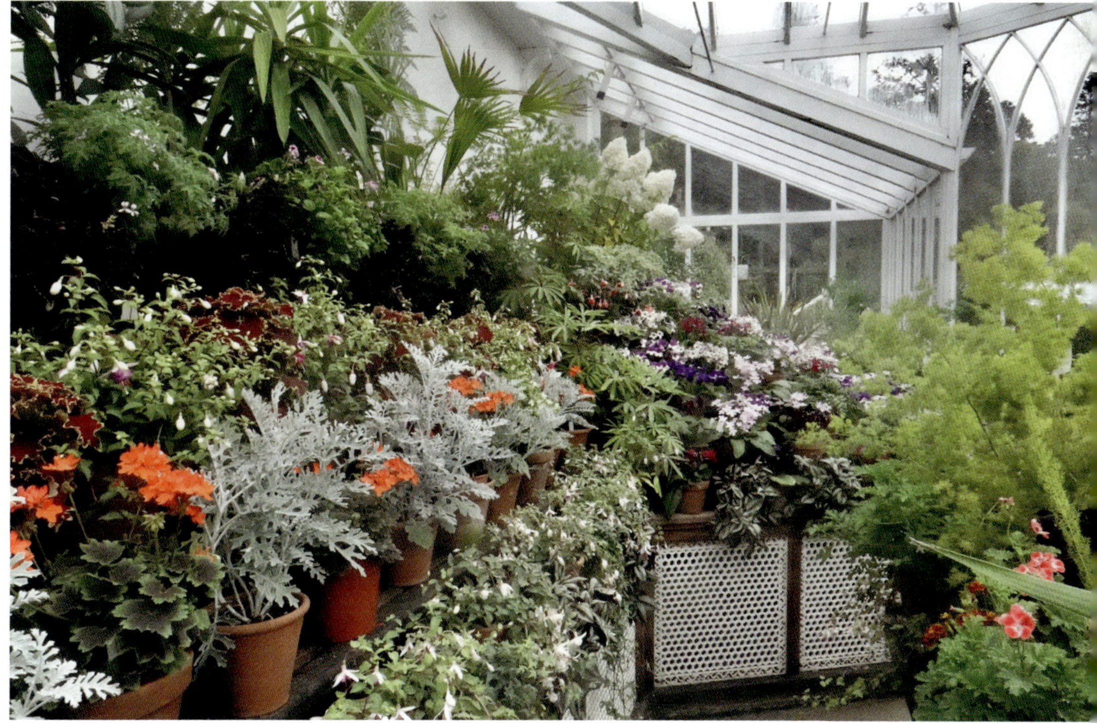

# The Estate Buildings

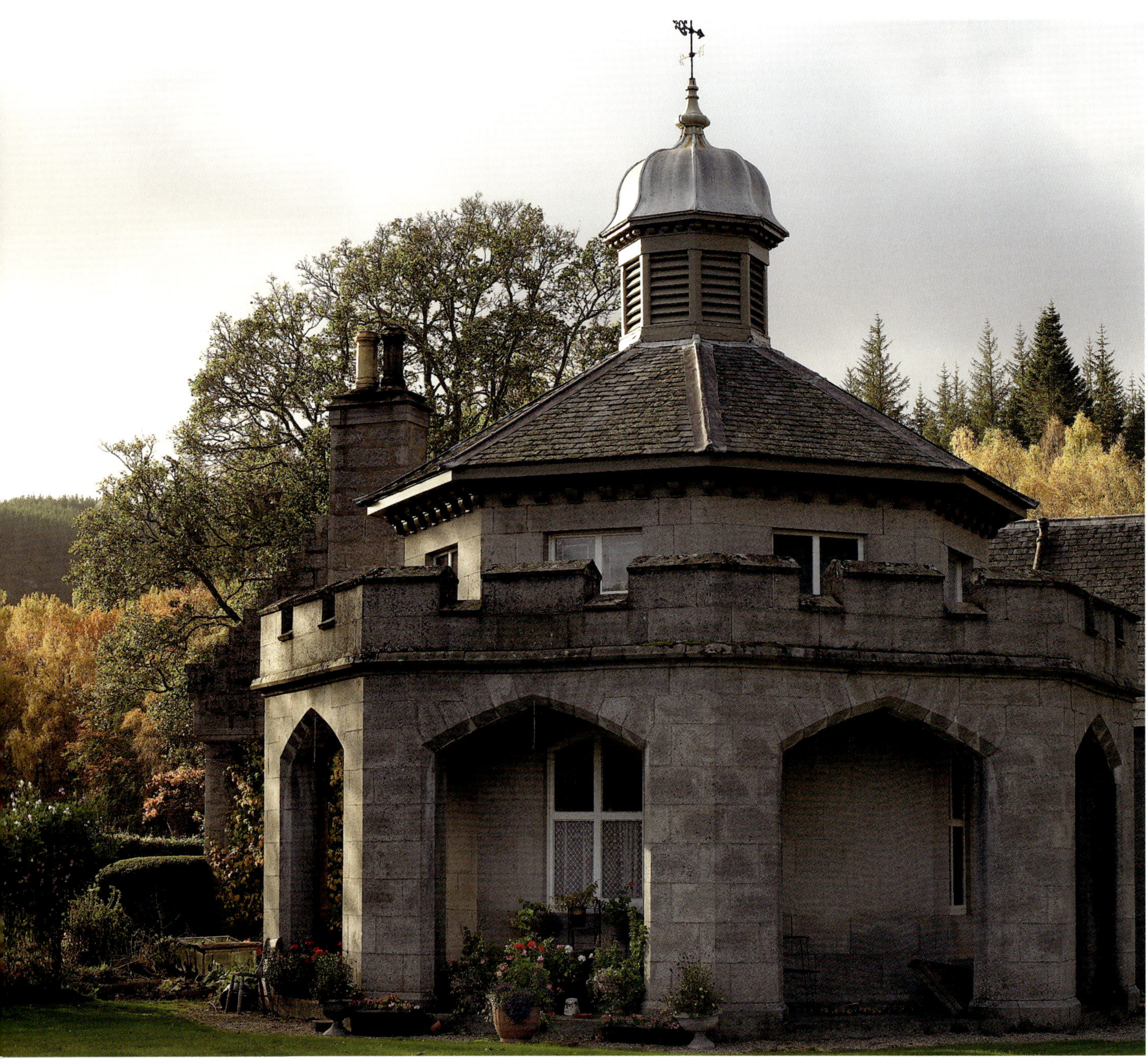

*left*  The dairy, designed by Smith with Prince Albert in 1861, comprised an octagonal pavilion with cottages and byre and was inspired by the model dairy at Frogmore, Windsor. Built in 1862–65, it remained in use until 1965.

*above right*  The picturesque venison and grouse larders, with pagoda roofs and ventilators. Designed by J. & W. Smith, 1850.

*below right*  Garden Cottage, built in 1863 and used by Queen Victoria as a quiet retreat; rebuilt in 1894–95 with barley-sugar chimney pots and rustic, tree-trunk columned veranda. The walls are harled concrete panels, the paintwork is in the estate colour, Balmoral Grey.

'Albert's … great taste, and the impress of his dear hand, have been stamped everywhere,' wrote Victoria proudly in her Journal on 13 October 1856. The following year, she noted that he was 'very busy superintending the plantations and laying out the grounds, which no one understands as well as he does'. She was right: the technical-minded Prince was ahead of his time in land management and Balmoral, which was in a run-down condition, presented an opportunity to exercise his ideas. In his final decade, he would transform it into a model estate.

Even as a tenant he had been busy improving – between 1849 and 1851, he added a service wing to the old castle and a venison larder, ice house, kennels, pony stables and iron-clad dancehall nearby. Committed to the welfare of his tenants, and keen to encourage good tradesmen and farmworkers to settle, he upgraded or built new cottages and two schools, stipulating that they should be plain and economically constructed. Today, Balmoral has about 86 estate houses, including nine holiday lets.

For the gate lodges and other prominent buildings, he engaged William Smith, who sustained his eclectic Scots-Tudor idiom – militarily severe for the granite-hewn complex comprising estate office, chauffeur's house, carriage house and stables (1857; now called the Mews); ornamental for the model dairy.

In the 1860s, a Tudorish pattern-book style of estate architecture appeared, seen for example at Invergelder farmhouse, by the clerk of works/ architect John Beaton. Other buildings erected

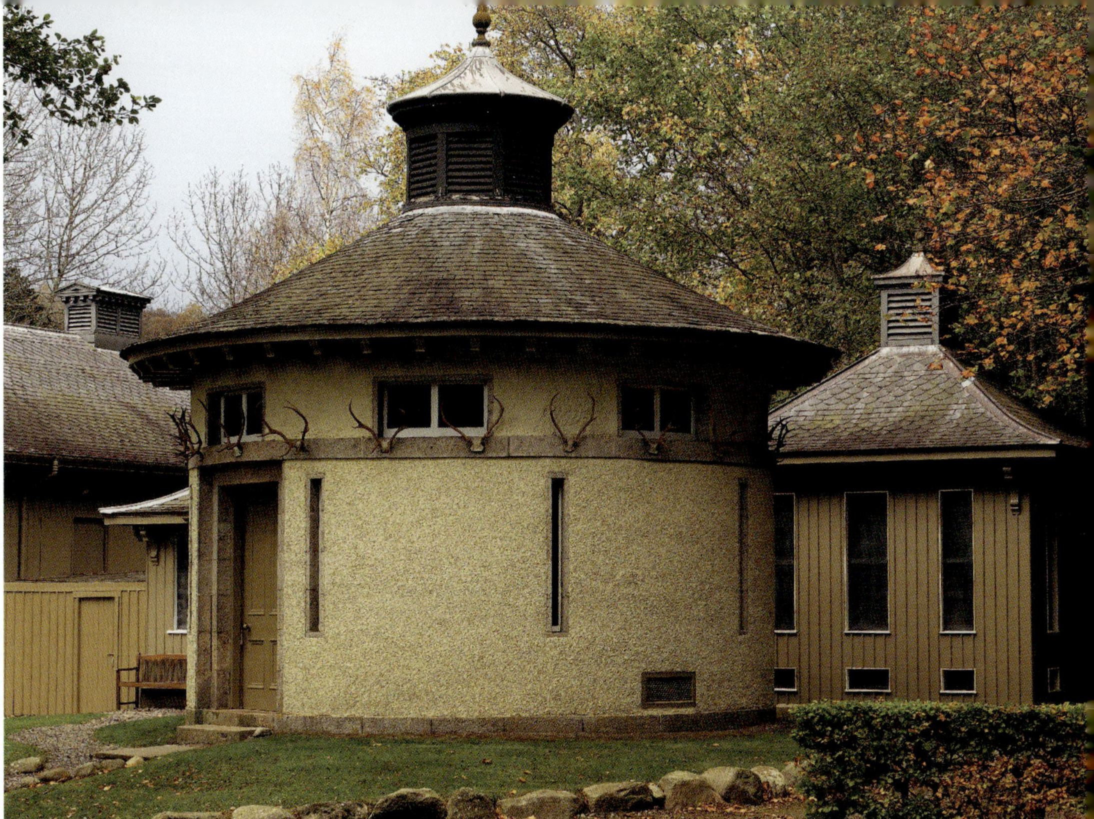

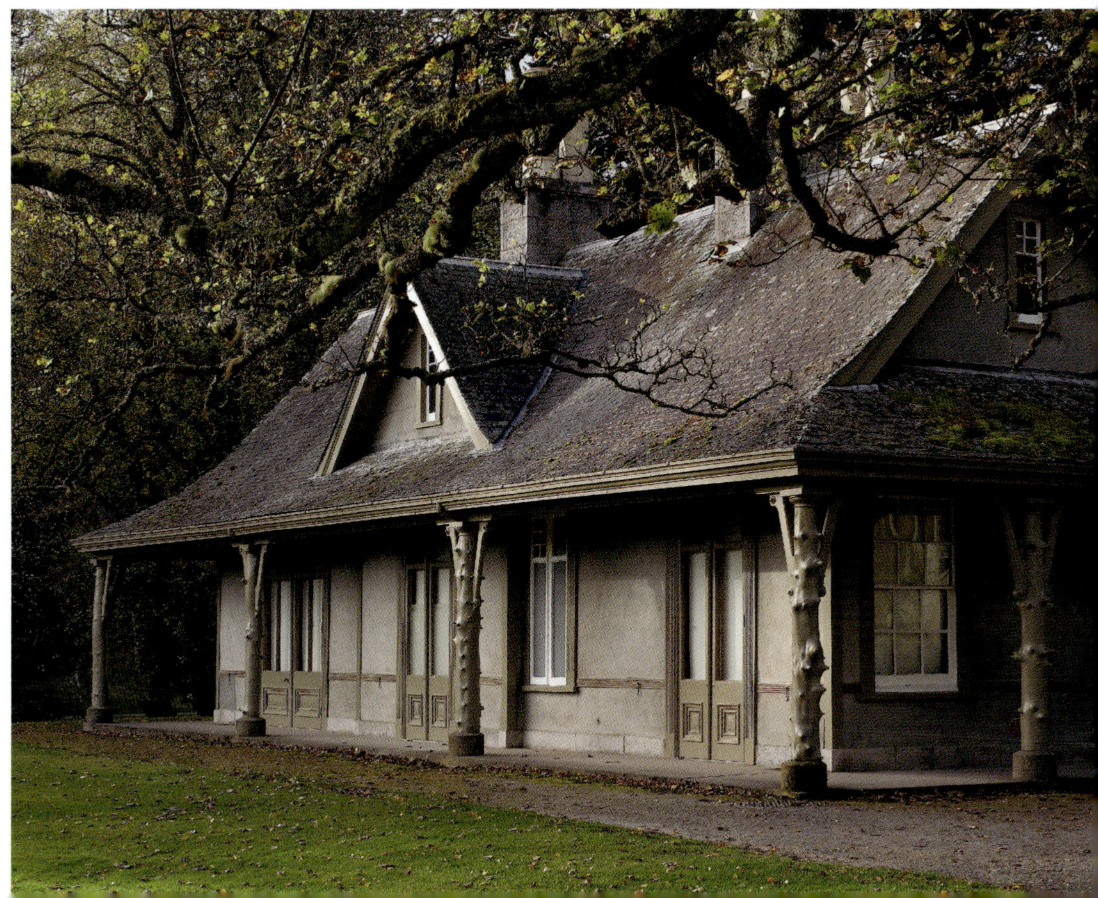

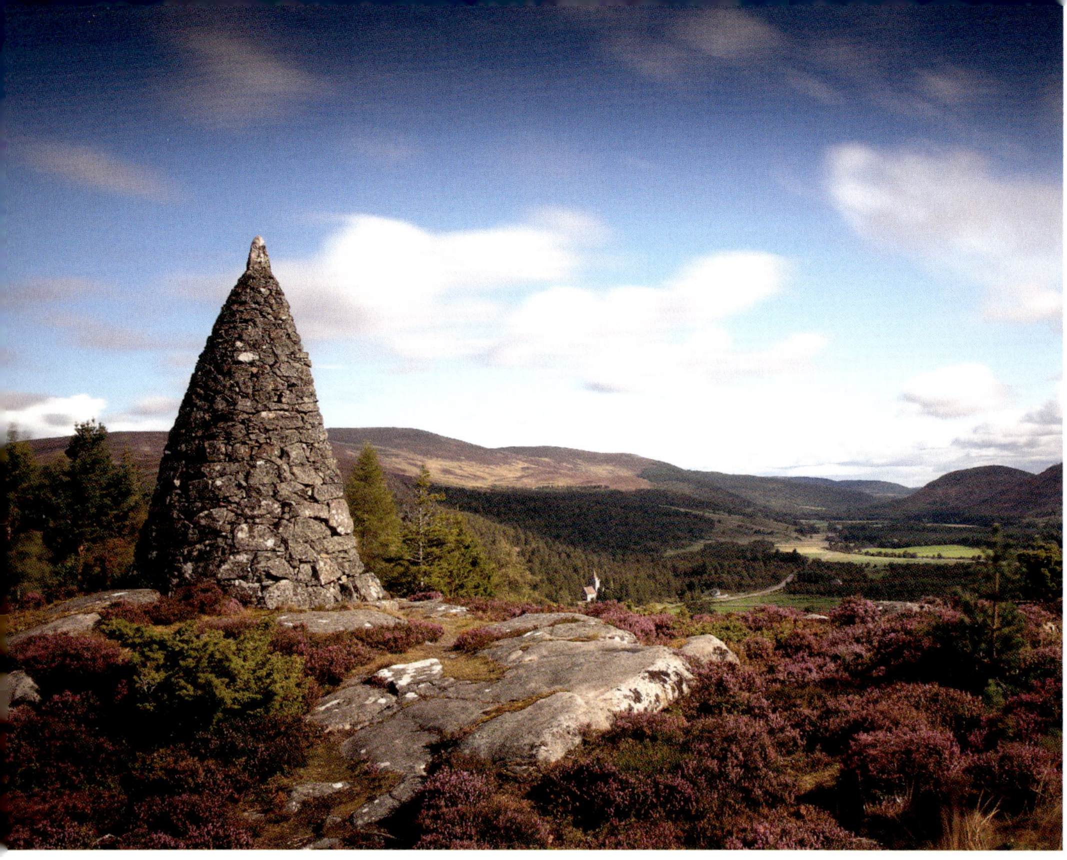

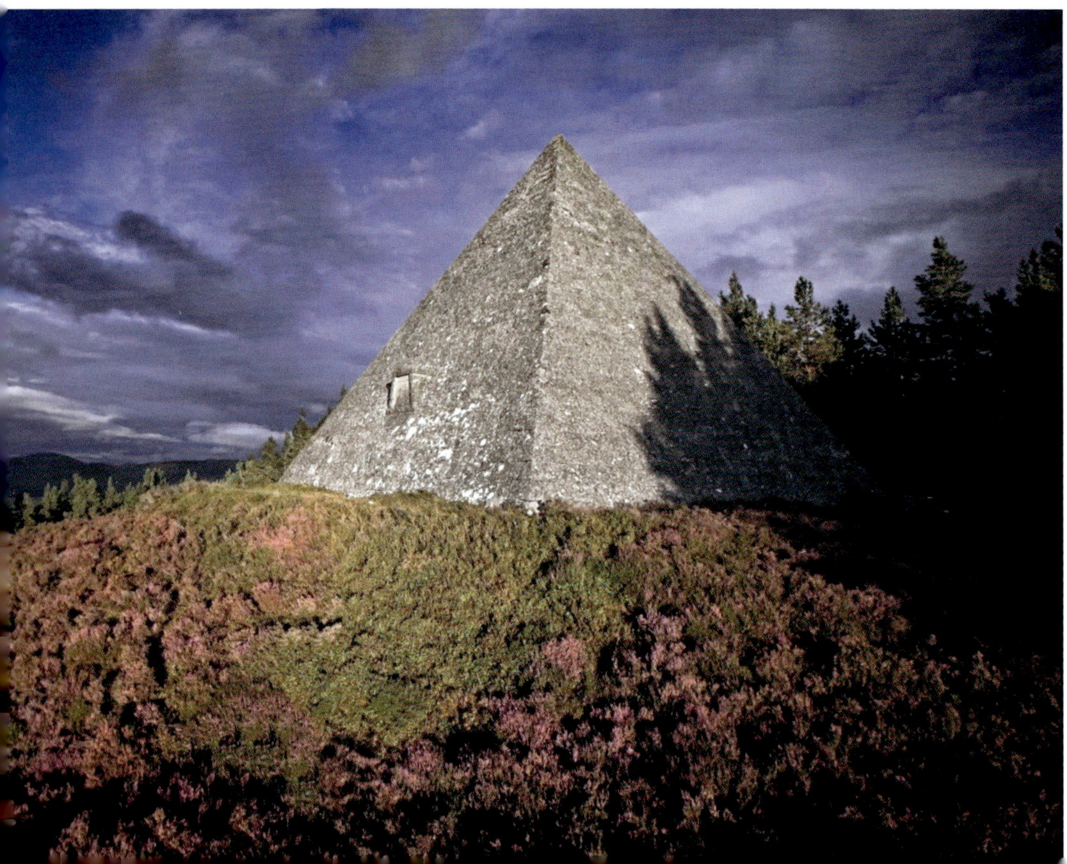

after Albert's death included Baile-na-Coille, now the factor's house, in a picturesque Tudor-cottage/chalet style; a bungalow for Abdul Karim, the Queen's Indian secretary (the *Munshi*); and several cottages, or 'shiels', used for picnics and remote escapes, such as the Danzig Shiel, where the Queen would sit cosily in a room 'entirely panelled with fine wood from the Balloch Buidh, the furniture also in pinewood, & the curtains & chairs Balmoral plaid', as deer came right up to the window.

Albert's landscaping included embanking the river, trenching and draining wasteland, followed by a programme of planting to provide much-needed shelter. The towering conifers shading the main approach and the mixed plantation on Craigowan were put in by him, as was what may be Scotland's earliest wrought-iron girder bridge (1856–57), designed by Brunel to take a road from Crathie over the Dee to the castle entrance.

A famous feature of the estate is its ensemble of commemorative cairns, statues, crosses and garden benches linked by a network of paths. The largest, a stone pyramid on Creag an Lurachain, is a monument to Prince Albert. Others commemorate the lives and marriages of his children.

Victoria and Albert are depicted in two bronzes: the Queen in state regalia by Boehm and an enlarged version of Theed's 1863 marble sculpture of the Prince, kilted with gun and dog (the original can be seen from the Red Corridor in the castle at the bottom of the main staircase). Also in their honour stand a pair of obelisks presented by tenants.

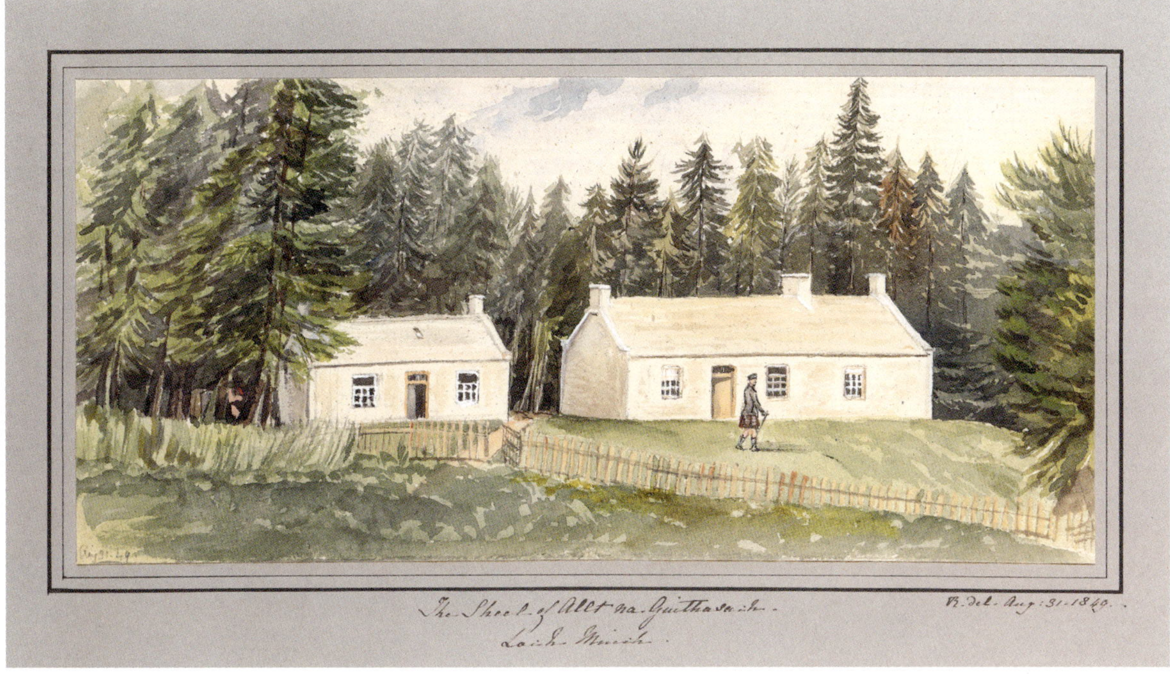



*opposite above*  The Purchase Cairn, built on the summit of Craigowan in 1852, to mark the purchase of Balmoral. Members of the family and household laid the stones amid much piping, reels and whisky.

*opposite below*  The Prince Albert Cairn on Creag an Lurachain. 'The good people here have subscribed £100 at their own expense, as a memorial to their dear Master. It is very touching,' wrote Queen Victoria.

*above right*  Queen Victoria's watercolour of Allt-na-Giubhsach, where she and the Prince Consort first stayed in 1849. They were enraptured by the wild setting in Glen Muick and by their simple, rustic existence when they escaped here. The King's current redecoration of the cottage for a holiday let is inspired by Victoria's descriptions of its cosy interior, and by a painting of 1863.

*below right*  William Simpson's 1882 watercolour of Glas-allt-Shiel, the house created in 1867–69 as a remote retreat for Queen Victoria in her widowhood. It was to this inaccessible spot that she would be rowed up Loch Muick to enjoy a few days of solitude in what had been Albert's favourite spot, always returning 'the better and the livelier for it', as her private secretary observed.

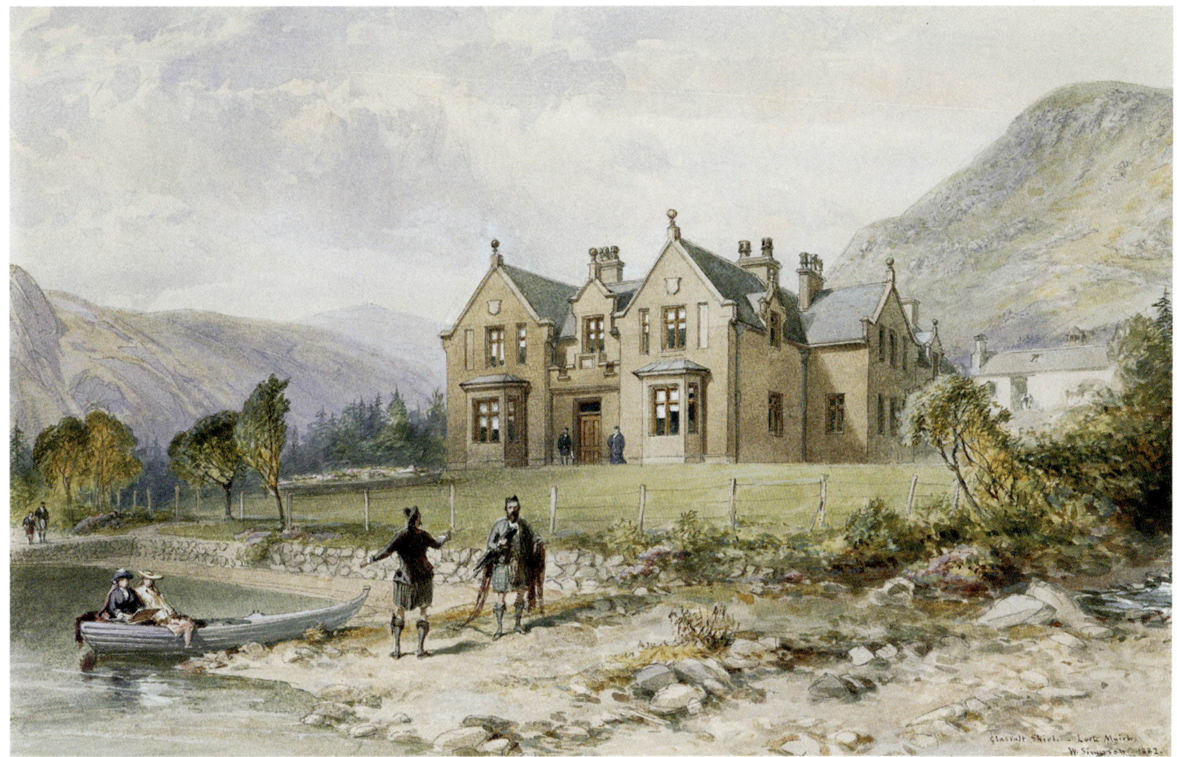

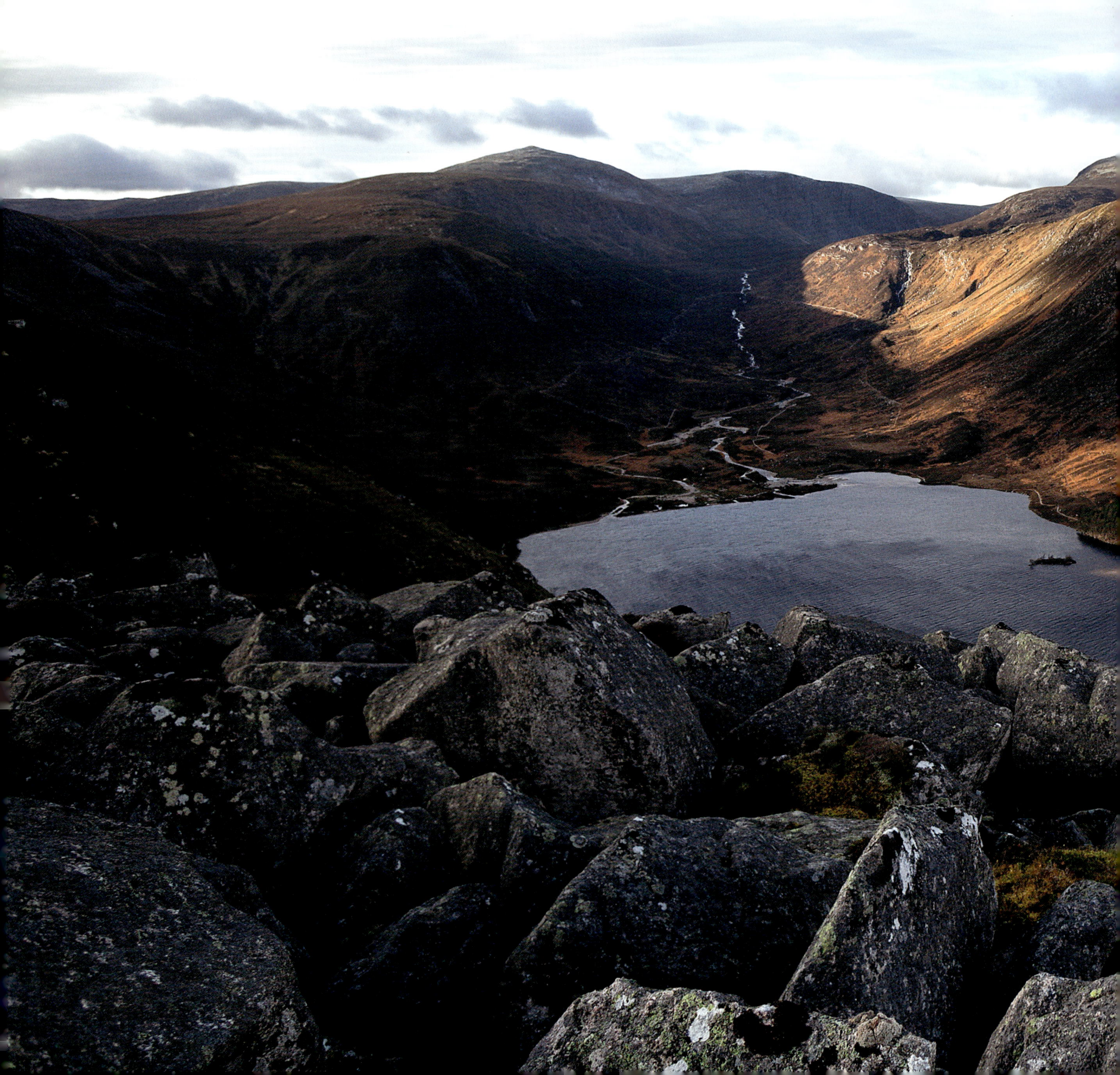

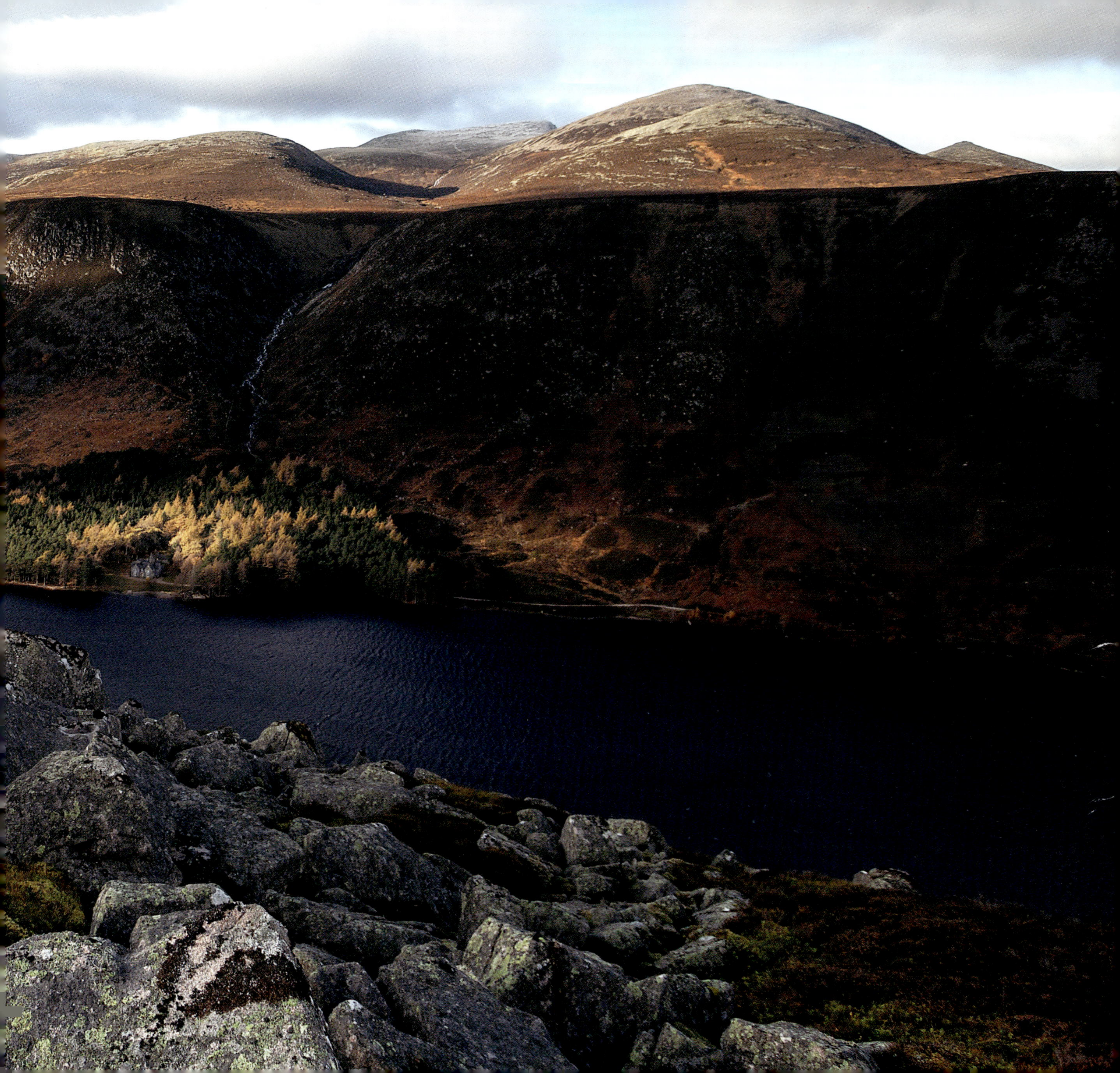

# The Wider Landscape

Bounded to the south by the glacial massif traditionally known as the Mounth, and stretching eight miles along the broad strath of the Dee, Balmoral's 50,000 acres encompass a diversity of terrains, from the rugged Cairngorm heights and ice-carved glens, heather uplands and tracts of pine and birch, to riverside pastures and the wooded policies of the castle.

Driven by The King's passion for the environment, the stewardship of this exhilarating landscape is focused on conservation and natural regeneration, with biodiversity the main emphasis. Projects include riparian planting, restoring peatlands and capercaillie, extending native woodlands and creating habitats for bugs and insects. Hydro schemes on the Muick and Gelder generate green energy.

The birdlife is rich and rare, and there is also a thriving population of mammals, principal among which are red deer, which require careful management to ensure a stable and healthy population. The Balmoral forest has six stalking beats, which are served by working Highland hill ponies. There are also grouse moors and salmon fishing beats on the River Dee, all managed by a full-time team of stalkers and gillies.

Pedigree Highland cattle, bred here since 1953, roam Ballochbuie woods, the ancient Caledonian pine forest that is slowly being regenerated. The estate has approximately 8,000 acres of trees, which are managed principally for conservation, with some commercial forestry and milling for use on the estate.



*previous pages* The glacial moraine at the south end of Glen Muick, which runs south for nine miles from Birkhall into the heart of the Cairngorms. Below Lochnagar, situated among trees on the shore of Loch Muick, is Glas-allt-Shiel (see p.73).

*right* One of the largest surviving remnants of ancient Caledonian pine forest, Ballochbuie was purchased by Queen Victoria in 1878. Col. Farquharson, whose ancestor had reputedly bartered the forest for a piece of tartan, had refused to sell, but eventually relented. The Queen paid £100,000 for it and erected a stone inscribed 'the bonniest plaid in Scotland'.

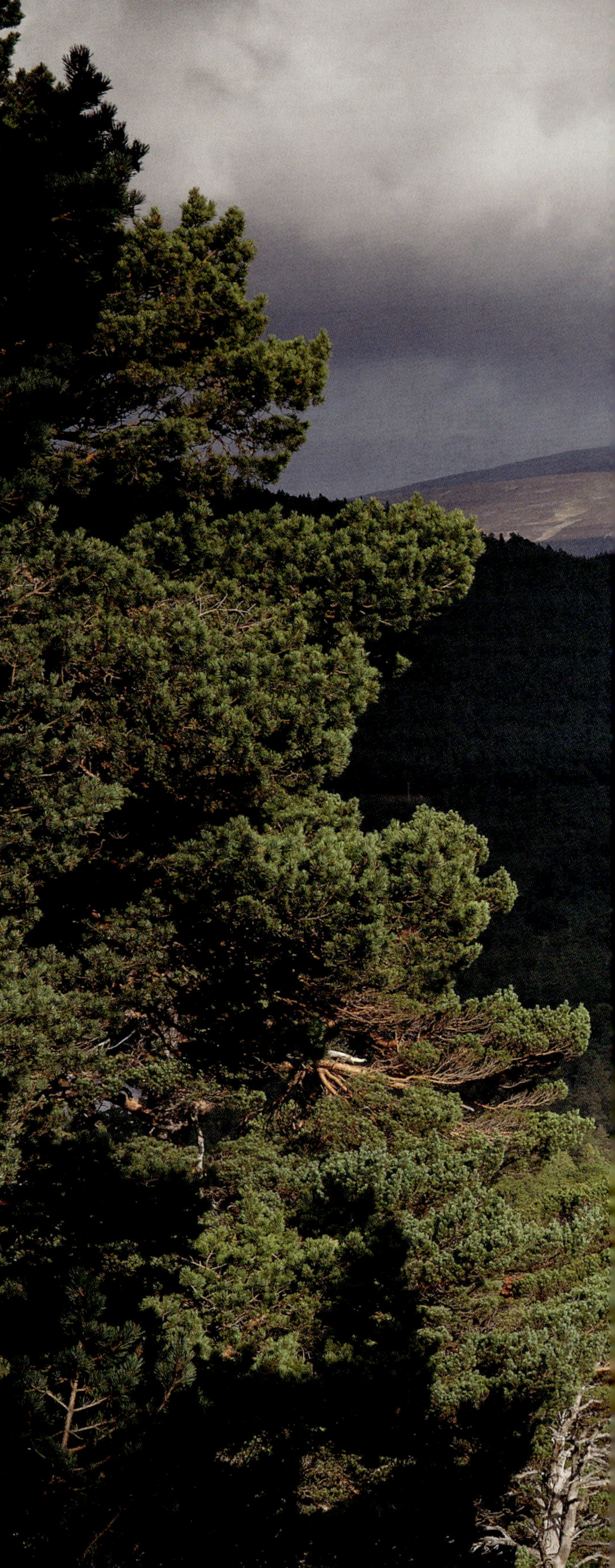

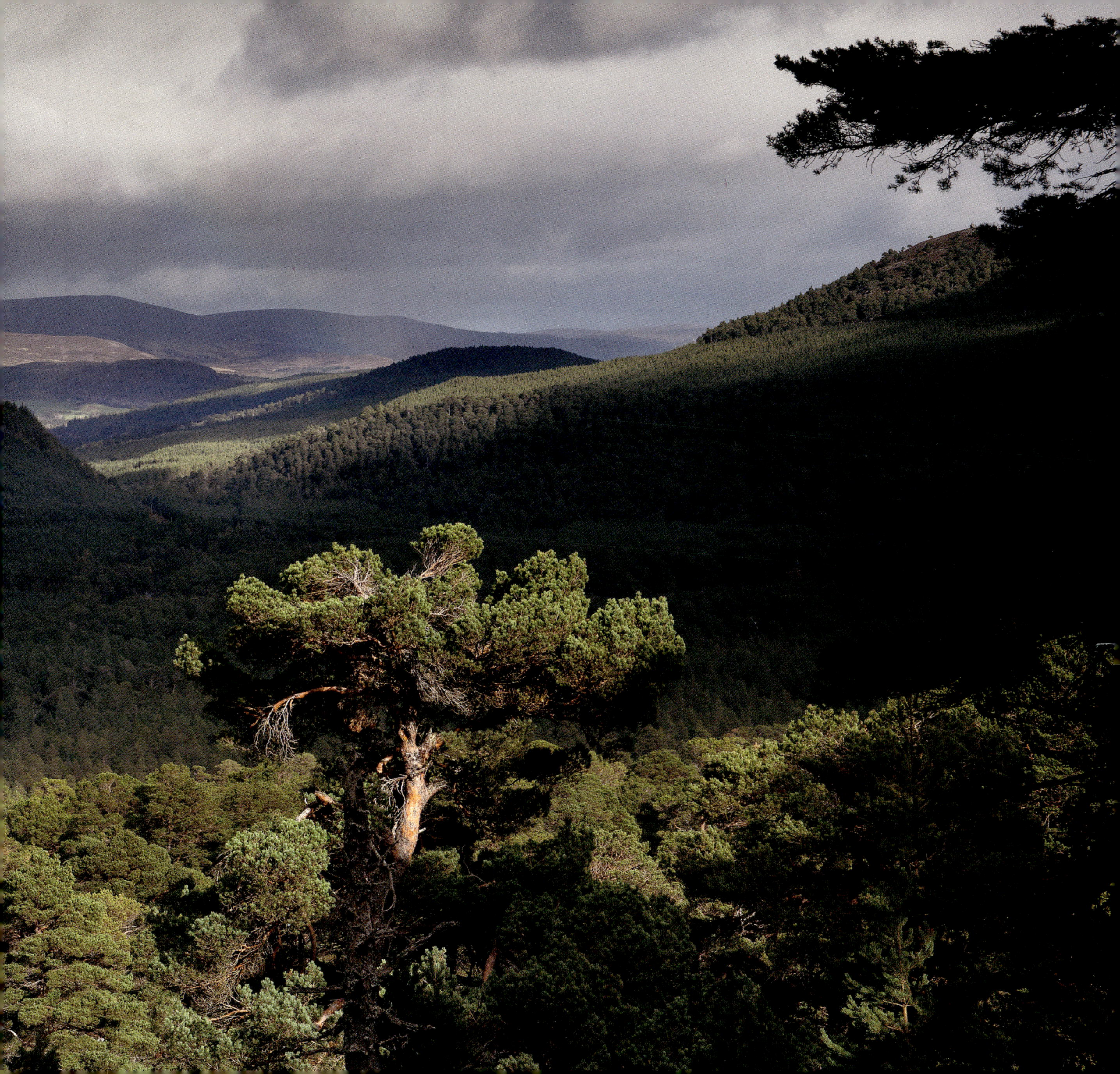

# The Braemar Gathering

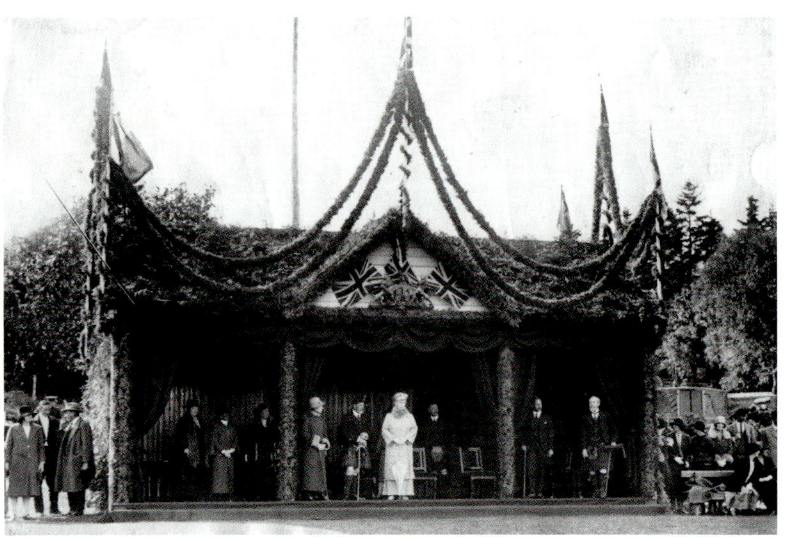

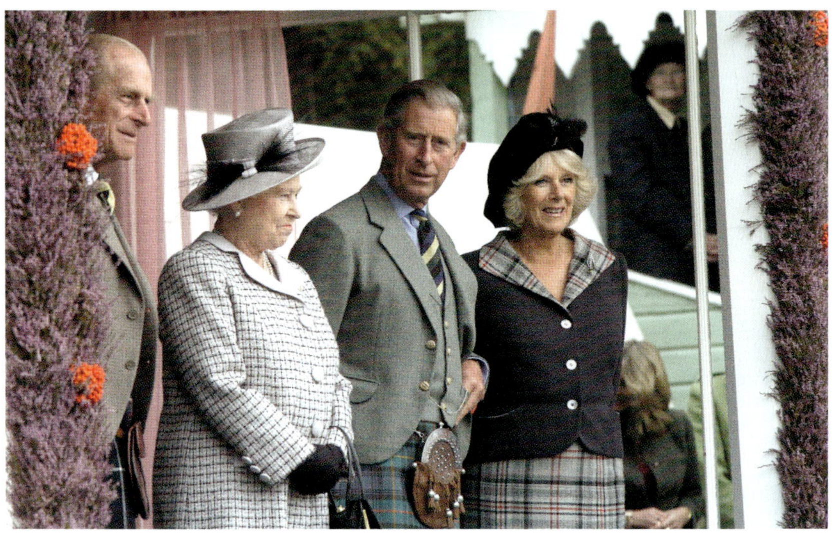

John Mitchell's watercolour sums up the pageant of tartanry, banners, piping and athletics that has become synonymous with the Royal Family on Deeside. Dating from 1832, the Braemar Gathering is rooted in the medieval tradition of the clan gathering, at which martial skills, athletics and the bagpipes demonstrated power and prestige. It evolved from an annual sporting event, established by a local Friendly Society that became the Braemar Highland Society in 1826. Widening its aims to preserve traditional customs and promote sport under the patronage of local landowners, the society held annual gatherings that reinterpreted aspects of Highland culture. Piping (integral to the old clan society) represented the military aspect; the sword dance and Highland fling re-created rituals of war; contests, such as tossing the caber, putting the stone, throwing the hammer and hill racing, revived ancient athletics. The muscular competitors fulfilled Queen Victoria's ideal of 'the finest race in the World'; 'it looked very pretty to see them run off in their different coloured kilts, with their white shirts (the jackets or doubtlets they take off for all the games)', she enthused after attending the Gathering at Braemar Castle in 1850.

The games were held at various places, including Balmoral, until 1906, when they were given a permanent site, the Princess Royal and Duke of Fife Memorial Park in Braemar. Since 1848, the reigning monarch has made a regular appearance as Chieftain of the Gathering, which is held on the first Saturday of September and has become one of Scotland's most famous tourist attractions.

*above left*  King George v and Queen Mary attending the Braemar Gathering. The rustic pavilion was replaced by the Duke of Rothesay Pavilion in 2019.

*above right*  The Gathering is an important fixture in Their Majesties' schedule when they are at Balmoral each summer.

*right*  Resplendent in Highland dress, spectators gather around the playing field in John Mitchell's 1898 watercolour, *Braemar Highland Games*. Held annually since 1832, the event triggered a craze for Highland games that spread throughout Scotland and the diaspora.

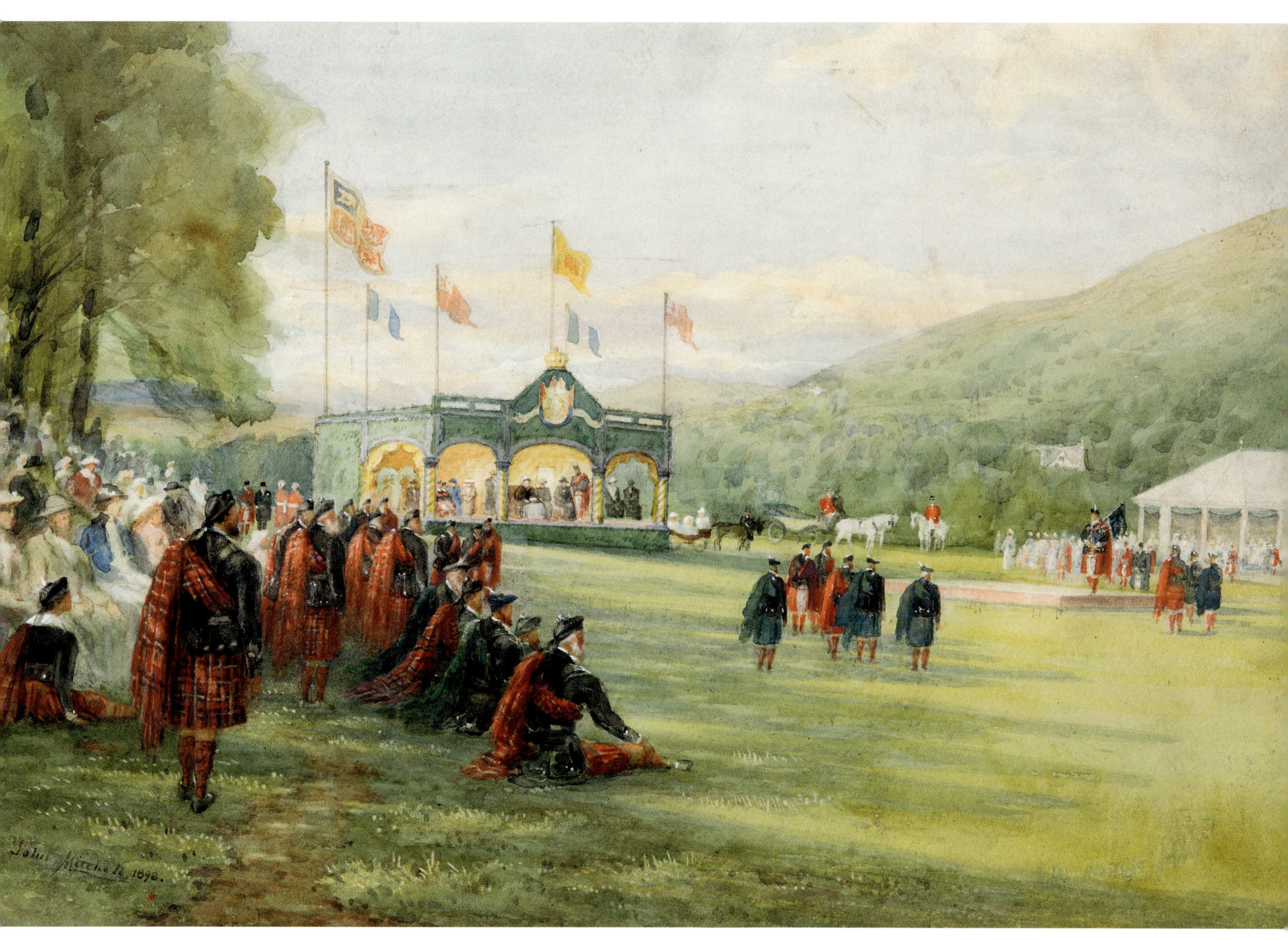

IMPRINT

First published in 2026 by Barbreck Publishers

Text by Mary Miers and photography by Christopher Simon Sykes
© HM King Charles III

This edition © Barbreck Publishers, 2026

ISBN 978-1-9995891-6-5



A CIP catalogue reference for this book is available from the British Library

Published in the United Kingdom by
Barbreck Publishers, 50 Albemarle Street, London W1S 4BD
and distributed by Penguin Random House UK,
One Embassy Gardens, 8 Viaduct Gardens, London, SW11 7BW

Designed and typeset in Miller by Robert Dalrymple
Printed and bound by Green Leaf Production, Slovenia

PHOTOGRAPHIC CREDITS



COVER IMAGE CAPTIONS

*front cover*  Balmoral Castle, photographed in September 2025.

*cover flaps*  The flock wallpaper designed by William Morris for Queen Victoria's Golden Jubilee in 1887, and put up in the principal circulation spaces at Balmoral. Featuring a crowned monogram and thistles in floral lozenges, it was block printed using a coloured mordant, or glue, on an ecru ground, on to which a fine merino wool flock was applied, brushed and laid. The VRI monogram signifies that Victoria was Empress of India as well as Queen of the United Kingdom. The wallpaper was reprinted by Sandersons in 1989 and now hangs in the Red Corridor, main staircase and Royal landing, as well as some secondary corridors and service areas.

*inside front cover*  Carl Haag, *Queen Victoria and Prince Albert Fording the Poll Tarf*, 1865. Haag's watercolour depicts an episode during the third of the four 'Great Expeditions' that Queen Victoria and Prince Albert made between 1860 and 1861, travelling incognito to scenic spots in the Cairngorms and staying overnight in local inns. This trip, which took place on 8–9 October 1861, was 'the pleasantest and most enjoyable expedition I *ever* made', Victoria wrote in her Journal. The party, which included Princess Alice and her fiancé Prince Louis of Hesse, travelled to Dalwhinnie for the night, and from there, via Blair Castle for a quick coffee stop, up Glen Tilt to the Falls of Tarf, where the Duke of Atholl 'offered to lead the pony on one side, and talked of Sandy for the other side, but I asked for Brown (whom I have far the most confidence in) … Sandy MacAra, the guide, and the two pipers went first, playing all the time … suddenly in the middle, where the current, from the fine, high, full falls, is very strong, it was nearly up to the men's waists.' They continued north to Bainoch (Bynack) Lodge, where they had a reviving cup of tea, before returning by carriage to Deeside, and back to Balmoral by moonlight. In 1864, the Queen summoned Haag to Balmoral to make studies for some 'pictures of dear Memories'. This painting, which overdramatises the falls, was exhibited at the Old Watercolour Society that year.

*inside back cover*  Plan of Balmoral Castle and the surrounding gardens and grounds.

*back cover*  The main entrance from the porte-cochère.